baby
on
board

This book is dedicated to my mother

Dorothy Kathleen Chilton

To acknowledge the wonderful
childhood I experienced, thanks to her
inexhaustible well of love.

baby on board

Understanding
what your baby needs

Dr Howard Chilton

FINCH PUBLISHING
SYDNEY

Baby on Board: Understanding what your baby needs
This edition first published in 2003 in Australia and New Zealand by Finch Publishing Pty Limited, PO Box 120, Lane Cove, NSW 1595, Australia. ABN 49 057 285 248
07 06 05   8 7 6 5 4 3

National Library of Australia Cataloguing-in-Publication entry
    Chilton, Howard.
    Baby on board: understanding what your baby needs.

    Bibliography.
    Includes index.
    ISBN 1 876451 39 4.

    1. Infants (Newborn) - Care. I. Title.
    649.122

Edited by Sarah Shrubb
Editorial assistance from Elaine Myors
Text designed and typeset in Slimbach by *DiZign* Pty Ltd
Cover design by Gas Creative
Cartoons: © 2002 Chris Morgan, cxmedia.com
Printed by BPA Print Group

Photo credits   Howard Chilton, Peter Doyle, Sean Doyle, Micky Foss, Bijay Kalsy, Mario and Kathleen Merlo, and Dawn Michel of Moving Images Photography.

For information on other Finch titles, see page 209

Contents

# Introduction

In the first few weeks, new parents have two big problems: lack of sleep, and helpful advice.

The first one goes with the territory; it's the second one that's tough. Something about babies brings out the helper in everyone. Little old men will stop young mothers in the shopping centre and give them advice on breastfeeding. And nothing can stop grandmothers …

Having been the Director of Newborn Care at a big maternity hospital in Sydney for over twenty years, I'm pretty good at giving advice myself. But I have discovered a better way. By giving parents a basic overview of how babies are designed, by explaining the origins and basic biology of their babies and the society they were expecting to be born into, we can enable parents to work out for themselves how to deal with their baby.

New parents need space and autonomy so that they can remain in control of their situation, but they also need information, so that they can enjoy parenthood and not worry unnecessarily.

We're all different. We all deal with situations in our lives in different ways, as a consequence of our conditioning and our circumstances. With parenting we carry messages that we gleaned during our childhood, and such messages subtly influence our attitudes and actions. So some mothers, for instance, should sleep with their babies; others would find this the road to disaster.

But having a basic understanding of how the persona of the baby is formed and how the little newcomer functions can help new parents work out the best way to manage their baby's care, without recourse to endless advice from friends or experts.

Howard Chilton
November 2002

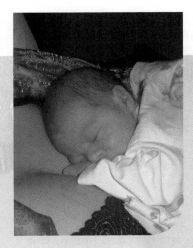

Day one: A quick 'set-up guide' to your new baby

(who's got time to read more?)

This is the information you might need on the day you have your new baby. You're tired and excited, have too many visitors, and certainly have no time for reading. If you just look at this couple of pages, you can leave the rest till later.

⋄ **Most babies are quite mucousy for their first 24 hours, some even having 'blue turns' when it sticks in their throat.**
Don't worry, babies are very good at getting fluid out of their airway. They're okay on their back and will not choke. Babies, as I will say many times in this book, are very well designed for birth and its aftermath.

◇ **Babies develop red weals on their skin in the first day or so. They can look like mosquito bites. These are more common in areas that are in contact with nappies or clothes.**

This rash is called 'erythema toxicum', and is a response of the skin to contact, especially with textiles such as cotton. It is harmless, not irritating and will go away without treatment. It does not mean your baby has an allergy.

◇ **Milk comes in at about two and a half days. Before that, babies are all over the place with their feeds, sometimes feeding constantly, sometimes sleeping for long periods.**

Your breasts produce only a dribble of colostrum for the first couple of days. So, for some babies, there's not a lot to wake up for. Let him do whatever he wants to do. The milk will come in anyway. Your job is to protect your nipples from damage from your baby's little mouth.

◇ **Get a midwife to help you attach the baby to the breast.**

Like other primates, our babies are not born with the correct breastfeeding technique – they need to learn to do it right. Until they learn, they can damage the skin of their mother's nipples.

◇ **When you feel your breasts changing and filling, it means there are about twelve hours until the arrival of the milk. Then your baby will start to feed frequently and greedily – he may seem insatiable (the 'feeding frenzy'). He'll be on and off the breast continually for 24 hours. Let him feed.**

Despite the way he behaves, he does not have a pain in his tummy, and he does not have wind. He just wants to feed and induce your milk flow. Let him.

◇ **Babies are 'marine animals' in the womb and are waterlogged when they are first born. They 'dry out' in the first few days and can lose up to 10 percent of their birth weight.**

That's why milk takes a few days to come in. Other animals' milk comes in with delivery, but humans need the delay to dry out. Don't worry about the weight loss. It's normal and it's only water.

◇ **There is no such thing as overfeeding your baby.**

Your baby is just trying to induce enough milk flow. Overfull babies vomit. It's okay.

⋄ **You can't cuddle your baby too much.**
Your baby has just left the warmth and security of your womb. He wonders where he is. He can't hear the familiar sound of your heartbeat that filled his life when nestling inside you. When he's upset, pick him up, cuddle him against your chest and put his ear against your heartbeat. He will settle.

⋄ **You can't spoil your baby at this age.**
Babies can't have too much, or too close, contact with their mother. They can't have too much attention. They cannot learn bad habits for months. Disregard all advice to the contrary.

> There's no such thing as overfeeding your baby

⋄ **Once the milk comes in, the snuffles and mucusiness may restart. Your baby does not have a cold.**
When your milk comes in the volume of milk increases enormously. The baby may 'siphon' the milk into his nose and sinuses. To protect the delicate mucous lining of these structures from the milk (or even gastric acid, if he vomits) the walls produce mucus. It can last for weeks, and after you go home, it may be worse at night.

⋄ **All babies vomit. However, they should not vomit bile.**
Regurgitation is normal in the baby. It doesn't mean he will suffer from reflux or that he is unwell. If he vomits bile (bright green vomit), he might need attention – call the staff.

⋄ **It's not blood in the urine.**
Most babies pass pink crystals of 'urate' in the urine in the first few days. The red stain in the nappy is not blood and is quite normal. It will go when the baby gets more fluid after the milk comes in.

⋄ **NEVER give up breastfeeding at 2 a.m.!**
Things often seem terrible in the middle of the night – in the light of day, most of them don't seem so bad. If you give up at night, when you're tired, upset and in pain and your baby's screaming non-stop, you may well wish you hadn't the next morning.

Make the decision in the cold light of day – this gives you a much better chance to make sure it's the right one!

⋄ **Babies do not need lots of sleep to grow.**
That's a myth. They grow anyway. Otherwise, the world would be full of midgets!

Myths and expectations

If you thought you received a lot of confusing advice during the pregnancy – just wait till you have the baby!

The mothercraft myth

Did you know that wearing a black bra will discolour your milk? That the treatment for the dry skin on the cheeks of a baby is the application of a baby's wet nappy? Or that a good way to get rid of the baby's 'wind' is to put her face down over a rolling pin and ro-o-o-oll out the wind, or perhaps massage her stomach with warm olive oil (in a clockwise direction)?

Nor did I, but these were pieces of advice given to very confused mothers from people close to them.

A really common one is the 'fact' that babies who don't sleep don't grow. You can imagine how relaxed that makes the household of an unsettled baby.

What is it that impels people to overwhelm vulnerable new parents with such obviously wrong, useless and usually conflicting advice? A couple of reasons spring to mind:

1 Blame the baby

Babies are enormously attractive. Not just human babies, but the young of all species are more attractive than the full-grown version. Let's face it, even baby crocodiles are cute, in a cold, reptilian sort of way. It seems that our brains are hardwired to find the shape and appearance of a baby's face attractive – a baby will bring out our desire to care and nurture. It gives us a surge of joy to help and get involved.

So being attractive is a powerful survival factor for the baby. It was even more so in the past, when childbirth was not very safe for the mother. Too often, before modern obstetrics, the mother did not survive the process, and the baby needed to find somebody to take her home and look after her.

Makeup and babies

It has been suggested that women's cosmetics and makeup are designed to simulate infant features on the adult face. So we make the eyes look bigger, the lips more bud-like, the nose less prominent, and the features and skin softer. Instinctively, this increases the attractiveness of the face.

2 It worked for me, so my experience is valuable for you

I was recently involved with the care of a baby whose mother is a successful city barrister, with a mind like a steel trap. She decided she would do her duty and breastfeed for six weeks before getting back to the real world. Time passed. At six months she thought the baby needed a little longer on the breast. At a year she was finding it very hard to contemplate going back to work. By then, to use her words, she believed that 'the baby was her greatest achievement'. If a woman of her intellect feels that way, it isn't very surprising that most mothers have a great desire to impart their hard-won maternal wisdom to new members of the sisterhood.

The point they miss, however, is that human babies are so tough and adaptable that there are 50,000 ways of doing it right, so it's not surprising that all this advice conflicts. The other problem is that each of these helpful bystanders has a personal investment in your doing it *their* way – this makes them feel good, and involved with your baby.

Now that you've been warned, you can deal with it. Smile and thank them, then ignore their advice.

Remember, babies are as tough as old boots, and are hard to mismanage if they're loved. So find one person you trust – and who knows what they're talking about – and listen only to that person. And trust your own instincts.

The way to look after a baby is by common sense and trial and error. Oh, and try to get enough sleep.

> I kept my arms down as much as possible throughout my pregnancy and had my husband lower all the kitchen shelves out of fear of strangling my baby with its own umbilical cord. A work colleague whose wife was also expecting had warned me of this. Some well-meaning person had warned my colleague's wife of this 'danger' early in her pregnancy and, being first-time mothers, we both took it to heart.

Expectations

Don't set your standards too high. I once had a 'celebrity patient'. Her baby got into minor trouble at birth by inhaling a bit of meconium (foetal stool) from the amniotic fluid. He puffed and panted and needed a bit of oxygen for a few hours. He remained in the special care nursery for three days and then joined his mother on the postnatal ward. Things did not go smoothly there either. There were feeding difficulties, sticky eyes, phototherapy for jaundice, a depressed mum – the works! Eventually everything sorted itself out and mother and baby went home in good shape.

ACTUALLY ETHEL...
BECAUSE I VALUE
YOUR ADVICE,
COULD YOU WRITE
IT DOWN AND PUT
IT ON THE PILE?

Imagine the position of my eyebrows when, a couple of months later, I picked up a women's magazine of enormous circulation to see a feature on this lady's experience of childbirth. She was evidently Earth Mother herself, from the spiritual delivery to the gentle lying-in, from the smooth breastfeeding to the quiet, satisfied baby at home. All was easy, fulfilling, natural and suffused with a warm, pink glow.

What a missed opportunity! If only she had told the vast readership the way it **really** was! How much more good it would have done. If only she had told of the agony as well as the ecstasy, the reality, not the idealised fantasy that somehow we have come to think of as normal.

It is not surprising, therefore, that some mothers go through pregnancy and into delivery with their expectations just a little too high. They are expecting a quick, painless delivery, and a perfect, beautiful, responsive infant who breastfeeds like a natural. This does occasionally occur – if it does, you're very lucky.

Alas, things are often not quite so picturesque. Contractions are a good deal more painful than the antenatal training might lead you to expect, although some women are just lucky and have an easier time than others. Not only do pain thresholds vary greatly, so does the actual power of the contractions. Do not allow someone else to tell you how much pain you ought to be able to cope with. There is no pain easier to bear than somebody else's! Feeling guilty about the need for analgesia is too common in labour wards and birth centres and is so unnecessary.

Labour should not be more painful than you can stand and your baby can only benefit if you are comfortable enough to relax and enjoy the experience.

Some babies also decide that labour is too hard and insist on being delivered by Caesarean section. In fact, this is over 20 percent of births in some urban populations. You should understand in advance that this might be necessary for you and your baby.

Many babies prefer to spend the first day or so sleeping, and are reluctant to feed. So your baby may virtually ignore you, even though you worked so hard to bring her into the world. Don't take it personally. When the milk comes in you'll regret thinking she was too quiet!

Just accept that labour, delivery and its aftermath may not be quite what you expect and don't set too high a standard for yourself or your baby.

> For a short time after I had my daughter, I used to get a bit jealous when I saw a pregnant woman at the shops. I grieved for the feeling of a baby in my tummy, so close and so much a part of me!

Attachment and bonding

Over the last several years a lot has been said and written about how we attach to and bond with our new baby. Lots of information is available about the factors that determine the ease or difficulty with which we open ourselves to the kind of unconditional love that a baby demands from us.

In animals less sophisticated than humans, the need a mother feels to care for her newborn is often triggered by a simple mechanism. If the mother immediately licks her new baby sheep or rat at birth and it remains with her for the first few days, she forms an unbreakable bond with the newborn that is rather more like imprinting than attachment. If this trigger does not occur, the relationship may never form, and the baby may never recover from this.

In humans the system is much more complex, with backup mechanisms that can come into play if the post-birth situation is not ideal. Careful scientific studies have shown that humans have great flexibility, and enormous ability to cope with adverse circumstances at birth – and after. However, the mother will probably have an easier time falling in love with her baby and feeling confident about meeting her needs after she goes home if all the following conditions – some of which mothers can change or plan themselves – apply:

◇ she had a happy, stable childhood
◇ she has a supportive partner
◇ the baby is a welcome addition
◇ she was conscious during her baby's birth, and the birth lived up to her expectations (and was not too painful)
◇ she then breastfeeds the baby early
◇ she has the baby in the room with her in the postnatal period.

> Certain factors make it easier to fall in love with your baby, but it will happen anyway

Missing any of those factors will make no difference, or very little difference, to a mother's attachment to her child in the long run. But in the early days it could mean that she has more difficulty getting to feel comfortable with her baby. The instinctive responses to look after her baby may flow less easily, and the process may take a little longer.

To enhance the experience of birth and promote circumstances that would encourage mothers to accept their babies into their lives more easily, the practice of obstetrics, led by Dr Leboyer and then others, moved towards the quiet, non-clinical atmosphere in the labour room about 30 years ago. This revolutionised birthing practice, and many mothers felt that their ability to bond with their babies was enhanced by the new practices. However, human flexibility is so great that it is hard to show any difference in the long term. It has been demonstrated in carefully controlled studies that after one year, there is no discernible difference – in the babies or their mothers – between Leboyer deliveries and routine deliveries.

So factors that enhance attachment should be encouraged, because they may make the task of getting to love your baby easier. But if you miss out on any of them – you may have a general anaesthetic for a Caesarean section, or your baby may have to spend 24 hours in the special care unit, for instance – don't worry. Your bond will be just as strong, and 'bond' is the right word. You're stuck for life.

It takes time to fall in love with your baby

This message was on a banner draped across the nursery in the hospital of the famous English paediatrician, Sir Hugh Jolly. He understood how many mothers worried that there they were, five days after the birth, and the baby was still 'just a baby'. No pink glow, no rending hearts, she's just a blob – and a noisy one at that. If you feel like that about your baby, be reassured that many other mothers feel just the same – and they too hate to admit the way they feel.

A study showed that over 30 percent of mothers still felt indifferent towards their baby after several days; some mothers took over a month before they felt comfortable with their baby. We are all different. We all deal with changes and accept new people into our lives at a different pace and in different ways. Give it at least a couple of months before you start to worry. Then if you can't stand her because she looks like a potato, perhaps you had better talk it over with your doctor, who will put you in touch with people who can help you. If you suspect that you are depressed and not letting your baby in because of that (see 'Postnatal depression' in Part IV), get help straight away.

My boy/girl twins were born at 36 weeks and were sent straight to the Nursery after I had a brief cuddle. In those days (1976) we were not allowed any contact with them during this time – we looked at them through the glass windows. When I started breastfeeding, my daughter had 'sticky' eyes for the first couple of weeks. They were puffy and closed, and I couldn't have eye contact with her. With my son it was different: he and I fell in love immediately. But with my daughter I really had to work at it. I am sure that if I had not breastfed, she would have been the baby I would have let other family members feed. It certainly took a lot longer to fall in love with her – but I did.

3

Your baby's birth experience

All the months of waiting are finally over. You've been to the antenatal classes, painted furniture, shopped for baby clothes and made endless plans. You have dreamed about the birth of your baby, and no doubt worried about how it would go; and then, after what seems like an eternity, the day finally arrives.

In the delivery room

As soon as a baby is born he will be examined to assess any difficulty he may be having converting from a dependent life inside the womb to an independent life outside. This examination will also find any important congenital abnormalities that need immediate management and treatment. The doctor or midwife can then assure the terrified parents that they can stop worrying!

It is at this time that the Apgar score is done. Five physical signs are scored either 1 or 2 (that is, total score out of 10) to assess how well he's adapting to life outside the womb and whether or not he has been affected by delivery. The baby is assessed at one minute after birth and again at five minutes after birth.

Apgar score
Performed at one and five minutes after delivery

Physical signs	Score 0	Score 1	Score 2
Heart rate	Absent	Less than 100	More than 100
Respiratory effort	Absent	Slow and irregular	Good and regular
Muscle tone	Limp	Some flexion of limbs	Active motion
Colour	Blue	Pink body, blue extremities	Completely pink
Reflex response	Nil	Grimace	Cough or sneeze to nasal catheter

The newly born baby

Sometimes newborn babies worry their parents by their strange appearance. Most of these odd characteristics are quite normal and will disappear sooner or later:

- ◇ swollen eyes
- ◇ throbbing fontanelle
- ◇ enlarged genitals
- ◇ rash of white spots over face
- ◇ changes in skin colour
- ◇ a coating of greasy white vernix
- ◇ fine hair over the lower back or shoulders (called lanugo)
- ◇ misshapen head (generally due to compression in the birth canal)
- ◇ swelling or bruising on the head as a result of the labour
- ◇ instrument marks (if there was a forceps delivery)
- ◇ turned-in feet

◇ bowed legs
◇ small, rather receding chin
◇ blue hands and feet
◇ swollen nipples
◇ ingrowing toenails
◇ rubbery lumps under the skin of the cheekbones and jaw
◇ red marks over the eyelids, nose and back of neck
◇ floppy, misshapen ears
◇ squashed nose
◇ crossed eyes (squint).

Newborn babies can look very strange

I was really upset when, straight after the birth, the whole family descended on the delivery suite. They were crowding around, taking the baby apart, 'his nose from Grandad', 'eyes from Auntie', even before my husband and I had had a chance to get a good look at her. I was so angry at their insensitivity – it drove me crazy.

Breathing

Within the womb the foetus floats in his ocean of amniotic fluid, supplied with oxygen and food from his mother's circulation through the placenta. His circulation bypasses the lungs through a couple of channels, one (called the **foramen ovale** or oval window) within the heart, and the other (called the **ductus arteriosus** or arterial channel) outside. His lungs are filled with fluid and, in the womb, are not used for absorbing oxygen.

The first breath

On delivery, many changes have to be made – your baby has to adapt to living independently on dry land. First, he needs to get rid of about half a cupful (125 ml/4 fl oz) of fluid from his lungs, and this he does – usually rapidly. A third of it is squeezed out into his mouth when his chest is compressed by the birth canal (in a vaginal birth) and the rest is absorbed into his circulation following the first breath. In a Caesarean delivery, his circulation must absorb all the fluid.

At the same time, under the combined stimulus of light, cool air on his cheek, a different noise level and a rise in blood oxygen caused by his first breath, his circulation undergoes radical change.

With the first breath the channels that bypass the lungs constrict and close and the blood vessels in the lungs open up. This forces the blood through the lungs on each circulation, where it absorbs oxygen from the air waiting in the lungs from the breath. This oxygen is then carried to the body. Normally, this process is rapid and smooth, and the baby requires no help.

Slow to start

Some babies terrify their parents by taking their own good time to start breathing after birth. These babies may be grateful for a little assistance. A little gentle suction of the mouth and throat, usually to remove mucus, blood or fluid from the lungs, sometimes provides an extra stimulus to the breathing drive. If this is not enough, the lungs can be inflated using a tight-fitting rubber mask and a ventilator bag. (This device is called a 'hand-bag' by some. Try not to panic when they say they 'hand-bagged' your baby!)

Most of the babies who require help will be stimulated by the inflating action of the mask to continue breathing on their own. Now and again, especially if the babies are sick or the lungs are not mature, more resuscitation is required. A tube the size of a drinking straw may be inserted into the baby's windpipe (intubation) and the lungs inflated directly with the ventilation bag.

Don't panic

It is important to remember how well designed babies are for delivery and how long they can manage without oxygen before there is any permanent harm done. A baby has to be totally without oxygen for at least 20 minutes before the brain is in danger of permanent harm. Should your baby's drive to start breathing at birth be depressed by lack of oxygen he will be given help to get things going long before he is in any danger.

If the ability of your baby's brain to withstand lack of oxygen has been stretched beyond its ability to compensate, your paediatrician will be able to detect it within 12–24 hours after birth. If this has happened, your baby will become progressively sicker over this time, before recovery starts. They don't immediately recover. So if your baby remains well during this time, he has clearly coped with the situation.

Wet lung

It has already been mentioned that a baby has about 125 ml of fluid in his lungs in the womb. Some babies are not very efficient at removing all this water from their lungs after delivery. They have less lung tissue available, so each breath is less efficient. These babies need to breathe faster in order to get the right amount of air in and out of their lungs per minute. Their respiratory rate, instead of being a slow and steady 40 times a minute, may be a rather more rapid 60 or 70.

Inhaled amniotic fluid

Another possible reason for rapid breathing after birth is the baby inhaling a little amniotic fluid before delivery. The result is the same. In medical parlance it is called 'transient tachypnoea' or 'wet lung', and it is probably the most common reason for otherwise healthy babies being admitted to an intensive care nursery after birth. In the nursery the baby is cared for, observed and occasionally given oxygen therapy. Usually the baby can get rid of the water in his lungs without any help within 24 hours – he can then return to his mother's side.

Infection

Unfortunately, there's a third possible reason for babies breathing fast after birth. Babies are very vulnerable to infection, and there is always the possibility that the baby has picked up a lung infection from germs in the birth canal during the delivery. Luckily, this problem is uncommon, but it is impossible to know straight away which few babies are infected. If there is *any* chance at all that the baby has an infection, the doctor will have a sample of blood taken and sent to the laboratory to be cultured for germs. The parents will know whether or not there is an infection in 48 hours. Meanwhile, the baby will be treated with antibiotics.

There is no question that this is the right way to approach this problem. However, it does mean that many uninfected babies receive antibiotics through an intravenous line for 48 hours – until the results of their blood cultures are known. Doctors are not so concerned about the antibiotics in themselves (they are commonly used for babies, cause no problems, and do not affect the baby's immunity); they are more concerned about the anxiety the parents feel, and the inconvenience of the intravenous drip.

If the cultures are negative, the antibiotics can safely be stopped straight away. If they are positive, the baby will need a full course of antibiotics, for a week or more.

Meconium staining

There is one group of babies that is given special attention at delivery. In over 10 percent of births, the amniotic fluid is stained with meconium (foetal stool). This can be seen before the baby appears. Meconium is a thick, treacly substance that is harmless as long as it doesn't get deep into the baby's lungs. If it does, it irritates the lining of the air passages and generally gums up the works. This can cause respiratory distress (breathlessness), pneumonia and other lung problems.

Consequently, when this baby's head emerges, his throat and nose are sucked out to remove any trace of meconium before he has had a chance to breathe. This will prevent him from inhaling it. If the meconium is difficult to remove he may be intubated at delivery to make sure that there is no meconium down his airway. This is good preventive medicine and will do him no harm.

Important infections around delivery

There are two potentially nasty infections that may be present around the time of delivery that are worth discussing in some detail: the group B beta haemolytic streptococcus and the herpes virus.

Beta strep

The first germ, known as beta strep or GBS, resides in the birth canal of 5–30 percent of women (it varies from area to area) and usually causes no problems. However, it can be passed on to the baby at birth, and one in 100 of these babies may become very sick. They may develop pneumonia, septicaemia and shock, and some may die – there is little that neonatal medicine can do to help them. Of course lesser degrees of the illness are also possible, and antibiotics and intensive care may rescue these babies.

Most obstetricians now check for the presence of this organism during the last trimester of pregnancy by culturing a swab taken from the vagina. If the organism is found, it can be eliminated by giving the mother a course of amoxycillin, or erythromycin if she is allergic to penicillin. However, it may return after a few weeks.

Many hospitals have carried out research to try to prevent the baby becoming infected during labour. These large studies of maternity hospital populations have shown that if the organism is proven or suspected to be present, giving the mother intravenous antibiotics early on in her labour reduces the likelihood of sickness in the babies to a very low level indeed.

When babies are infected by this organism, the first sign of illness after birth is usually respiratory distress (breathlessness). Consequently, most babies with this symptom are treated with antibiotics immediately, just to cover the possibility of infection (see 'Wet lung').

Herpes

A significant proportion of women nowadays carry the organism causing the second potentially nasty infection: the herpes virus. This causes recurrent ulcers in the genital tract, especially around the vulva. These sores may last for three to five days and then heal completely. However, they may come and go for years. Another common condition caused by the herpes virus is cold sores on the lips. This is a different species of the virus, but for all practical purposes it is the same.

If babies are infected with herpes, usually by direct contact with an ulcer, it can be a devastating disease. They can suffer recurrent skin infections, brain damage – they can even die. Luckily, such infection is quite rare, despite the virus being common in mothers.

The reason for the rarity of the disease in newborns seems to be that the mother's antibodies travel to the baby through the placenta and protect him against catching the herpes infection. These antibodies (like all antibodies transferred from the mother) disappear from the baby's circulation within three months, but they work very well at birth, when the baby may be in contact with herpes ulcers in the birth canal.

A few years ago obstetricians were so frightened of babies catching herpes from a recurrent ulcer that a Caesarean section was performed if an ulcer was present. We now know that the danger is extremely low, so vaginal delivery is now back as an option in these cases.

Of course the baby is still very vulnerable if the delivery occurs when the mother is having her very first attack of herpes ulcers. If this is the case, the mother has no antibodies to give the baby protection – up to half the babies delivered in these circumstances would probably catch the infection, so a Caesarean section is absolutely necessary here.

Another important point to remember is that the herpes antibodies in the baby's circulation wear out after a few months. So later on, if the mother suffers a herpes attack, she really needs to maintain careful hygiene – she must wash her hands carefully and take care not to put the baby in contact with the ulcers.

Similarly, if the baby's mother has **not** had herpes, then the baby has no antibodies and is very vulnerable to catching the virus, so cold sores on the lips of his father, friends and relations can be a real danger. This is the commonest source of the virus in babies who catch herpes. It is most important to keep the baby away from active cold sores.

Other organisms

There are other organisms that can cause infections of the baby if they are present in the birth canal at the time of birth. There are two common sexually transmitted germs that can either cause overt infection or lie dormant on the cervix or in the vagina and still cause problems for the baby: gonorrhoea can cause septicaemia and severe eye infection, and chlamydia can cause eye and lung infection.

If you think there is a possibility that you may have been exposed to either gonorrhoea or chlamydia, let your doctor know so that you can be tested.

Genital warts usually don't infect babies, although the occasional case has been reported.

The commonest infection in the vagina during pregnancy is thrush. This causes few, if any, problems for the baby. Some babies may get a mild infection in their mouth, but there are many other sources of the fungus besides their mother.

Finally, if you are a carrier of the hepatitis B virus, your baby is vulnerable. Nowadays he can be completely protected by getting both active and passive immunisation. An injection of an antibody (HBIG or hepatitis B immunoglobulin) soon after birth will protect him for the first few weeks. He should also have the first of a course of hepatitis B vaccine injections. He will then get the full course as part of his routine immunisations, which are done at two, four and six months.

Vitamin K

Soon after your baby is born, he will be offered an injection of vitamin K. This practice is pretty universal, and for good reason.

Until 30 years ago there was an important, common and potentially lethal condition of babies called 'haemorrhagic disease of the newborn', which affected up to 1.5 percent of babies. Typically, a few days after delivery, the baby's blood clotting system would cease to work efficiently, and bleeding, often severe, would occur from the umbilical cord or the bowel.

The baby would often recover spontaneously if the haemorrhage was minor, but if the blood loss was heavier, he could rapidly go into shock caused by blood loss, and, unless treated, could die. The treatment was blood transfusion and vitamin K.

What does vitamin K do?

The blood-clotting system of the body is based on a complex series of reactions between many proteins and chemicals called clotting factors. Many of these require vitamin K for their activation – without it, there is poor coagulation (clotting). When this was realised, a routine injection of vitamin K after birth became commonplace, and the disease virtually disappeared.

That is, until the last fifteen years or so. Since then there have been reports of a new and deadlier form of haemorrhagic disease. This form occurs later, about four to six weeks after delivery, and the bleeding is often in the brain. This has serious consequences. These babies have two things in common:

> When vitamin K injections after birth were routine, haemorrhagic disease virtually disappeared

◇ They did not receive vitamin K after birth.
◇ They were all exclusively breastfed (no formula at all).

Studies have shown that many healthy babies born at full term have only marginally satisfactory stores of vitamin K. By the third day of life, as they start to grow, they can already have a vitamin K deficiency. Giving vitamin K to the mother before delivery does not seem to help, as it doesn't pass across the placenta well.

We also know that breastmilk contains only very small amounts of vitamin K. Cow's milk and commercial infant formula have very much higher levels than breastmilk (up to ten times as much). If a nursing mother is supplied with adequate vitamin K in her diet, a little will appear in her milk and be absorbed by the baby, but nowhere near enough to prevent haemorrhagic disease. If you are breastfeeding, it is a good idea to eat some fresh green leafy vegetables every day, as these are a rich source of this important vitamin.

Why has haemorrhagic disease reappeared?

There are probably two reasons:

◇ With the movement against technology in birthing and the 'cancer' scare (discussed below), some parents refuse the vitamin K that is offered to their baby.

◇ A few years ago most babies received at least a little formula or cow's milk as supplement, even when fully breastfed, and this was enough to boost the baby's vitamin K level and avoid deficiency. Nowadays, anxiety about cow's milk allergy means it is more likely that he will receive no such supplement.

The administration of vitamin K

For over 20 years most of the developed world has been giving an injection of 1 mg of vitamin K to all babies at birth. This completely eliminated haemorrhagic disease in newborns and apparently had no side effects and was not dangerous.

In 1992 a study from England was published which claimed to show that there was a remote possibility that this injection might double the risk of childhood cancer in those who received it. There did not seem to be any added risk for those babies who received vitamin K by mouth. There were many technical problems with this study. The article reported that the authors had gone back over the records of a group of babies who were born some 20 years before and who had received an injection of vitamin K. They had tried to compare this group with a similar group of babies who did not receive vitamin K, or who received it orally. Even the authors of the study pointed out the shortcomings of their work.

In addition, there was virtually no logical basis for believing the conclusion. There is very little indication that vitamin K has any relationship to anything other than blood clotting – least of all to cancer.

However, the most powerful argument against the conclusion is the leukaemia statistics from countries that have used the injection for 20 years or so. The incidence of leukemia has not changed at all, anywhere. It has stayed at a level of about four per 100,000 (up to four years), and seven per 100,000 (five to nine years) since the late 1940s. This is shown in statistics from the USA, the UK and elsewhere, including Australia.

A persuasive and exhaustive study done in Sweden in response to the English study produced the final answer. The study looked at data from 1.3 million infants born over a 16-year period: one million were given vitamin K by injection, and the rest were given it orally. The authors could not find any difference in cancer or leukaemia statistics: the injection was found 'not guilty'.

When the uproar started there was a swing away from injection to oral vitamin K in some countries. Unfortunately, even the new oral preparation needs to be given in at least three separate doses to come close to the reliability of the injection.

Some authorities suggest that even if the English study's conclusions are untrue, it is a good idea for vitamin K to be given orally. They recommend that babies receive 2 mg of vitamin K orally on day one, day four and again at four weeks of age (some recommend giving it monthly until solids are introduced). This is still only **nearly** as reliable as the injection. And the danger with this is, of course, that if all doses are not taken there is still a risk of the baby developing haemorrhagic disease.

Other authorities, such as the American Academy of Pediatrics (which, I might add, belongs to the most litigious and cancer-phobic society on Earth), suggest no change to present practice.

There is little doubt, now that the shouting and arm-waving have stopped and we have reliable information, that an injection of 1 mg of vitamin K is the safest way for your baby to be protected.

Under-standing your new baby's body

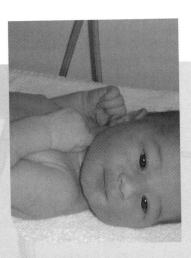

E very newborn infant should have a thorough physical examination early on in her life. During her stay in hospital the baby will usually have at least two or three physical examinations.

Full physical examination

When the baby has settled down and is warm, dry and comfortable, a paediatrician will examine her thoroughly.

Observation

A paediatrician can get lots of information about the baby merely by observing her. Following this general look, a more specific examination can be conducted.

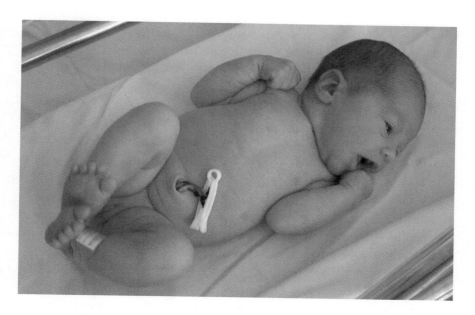

Posture. The baby usually lies in a relaxed posture, with arms by her sides, elbows bent, hips and knees flexed. Her body is straight, and her head is on one side (see photo).

Colour. Her colour is generally pink (rather darker in Negroid babies), but her hands and feet may be blue and cool for the first few days. After two or three days her colour may become slightly yellowish as the normal jaundice occurs.

Breathing. She breathes quietly, at a rate of about 40 breaths a minute, but may also have a pattern of alternate panting and shallow breathing – this is normal for the first three months of life.

Facial appearance. Her face is examined to see whether it seems to have a normal appearance (if it seems a little unusual, the paediatrician will usually have a look at Dad before saying so!).

Skin

Straight after birth, the skin of a newborn looks very pink, even red, because the haemoglobin level – the red pigment in the blood – is high during foetal life.

Maturity

◇ The thickness of the skin relates to the baby's maturity. A baby born early has fine, pink, delicate skin; the skin of a post-mature baby (a baby born two weeks or more after term) has a pale, scaly, parchment-like appearance.

◇ White, greasy material, called vernix, may be present (especially in the skin creases), in all babies, but is particularly likely in those born more than a week or two early.

Birthmarks

◇ Most babies have so-called 'stork-bites', which are flat red birthmarks over the eyelids, bridge of the nose and back of the neck. The ones on the face disappear over the first year or so.

◇ 'Mongolian spots' are irregular areas of deep blue pigmentation, usually found above or around the buttocks. They occur in all races, but especially in Asians, and they mostly fade over the first few years.

◇ Port-wine stains, which are deep red flat birthmarks that can be quite large, are more unusual. They don't disappear unless they are treated, usually with laser therapy.

◇ Strawberry marks – bright cherry-red, protruding marks – tend to arise a week or two after birth (see photo, page 25). They can grow larger for about eight months, but will eventually disappear (without treatment) between the ages of five and ten.

Milia

These little white spots (like millet seeds – hence the name) are due to swollen sweat glands, and are mostly seen over the cheeks, chin and nose. They are probably caused by hormones from the placenta interacting with the developing sweat gland. Don't worry about them, even if they increase in number – they disappear after the first few weeks.

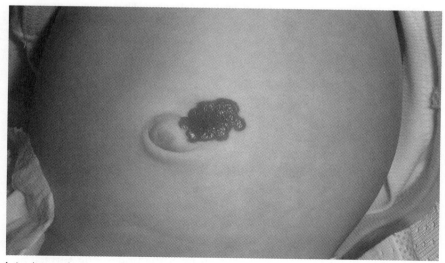

A strawberry mark

Other marks

Some babies have bruises and other marks from the delivery, especially on their heads and faces. Have no fear, babies are designed beautifully for what they have to go through (you!), and they heal very rapidly. Within a couple of days most of the marks will have gone.

Don't get upset about forceps marks or the mark from a suction cap (Ventouse). Forceps have got a bad name quite unfairly. A forceps delivery is actually preferred by many paediatricians for premature babies. The forceps act as a protective cage around the soft skull. Used properly, they do good, not harm. They are primarily used to guide the head of the baby through the curved lower part of the mother's pelvis if progress is slow, the head is in the wrong position or the mother is too tired to push.

The head

The paediatrician will measure the head circumference and feel the fontanelle (the soft spot at the top of the skull) and the edges of the skull bones.

Head shape

◇ Babies are a bit like toothpaste in their ability to fit through tight places. Following delivery, particularly when the birth canal is narrow, the baby's head may be elongated and misshapen. This is very common. My only advice is to stop worrying and wait a while before taking the first baby photographs.

◇ Babies' skull bones (there are four over the vault of the head) are not fused and can override each other to allow the head to pass down the birth canal. This overriding, or moulding can appear as a thickening over the midline of the skull or above the ears. It disappears in the first few days and no harm comes to the brain underneath.

◇ The head may also develop caput, a boggy, irregular swelling of the soft tissues of the skull, again due to compression by the birth canal during labour. After a few days the swelling will disappear.

◇ The bone may also become swollen. Bone has a membrane (called the periosteum) stuck firmly down to its surface. If the flat skull bone is flexed a little or sucked by a Ventouse (vacuum) suction cap to help delivery, this membrane may split off from the underlying surface and there may be bleeding underneath it. This gives a soft boggy swelling called a cephalhaematoma, which takes a few weeks to disappear. In 20 percent of cases the swelling turns to bone and the skull shape remodels over a longer period of time – but it does disappear eventually.

The fontanelle

This is a diamond-shaped soft spot at the top of the head that is easily indented with the finger. Despite its apparent vulnerability, it is a very thick, tough membrane and there is no danger at all of injuring your baby with normal handling. It often gets a little larger in the first few months – it will close between the ages of nine and eighteen months.

◇ You may notice that it sometimes pulsates with the heartbeat: this is normal. It also bulges when the baby cries or strains. This is normal if the bulging goes away when the baby stops screaming or is sat upright.

◇ Sitting babies up will make their fontanelle either flat or sunken. Again, this is not a problem. You may have heard that a sunken fontanelle can be related to dehydration. It is indeed an important sign of dehydration, but it is a very late sign, and the dehydration would have to be severe – you would have noticed other symptoms well before this. If the baby is wetting more than three nappies a day and isn't obviously ill and dry, don't worry. A sunken fontanelle does not mean anything on its own.

The eyes

These are usually clear, blue–grey or brown. For most babies it takes about a year for the final eye colour to be revealed.

> It usually takes about a year for baby's final eye colour to be revealed

◇ Small spots of blood within the white of the eye are very common. They are due to the bursting of capillaries from the compression during labour. They are completely harmless and disappear in a week or so.

◇ An intermittent squint is also normal, especially when the baby feeds, because babies only use the image from one eye at a time – the other eye's gaze may wander off. Unless the squint is constant, there is no cause for concern. Remember, babies see clearly from birth and indeed have an early preference to look at faces.

The mouth

◇ Small white cysts are frequently seen along the gum margins and on the hard palate, especially in the midline (the middle of the palate). They are of no consequence and will soon disappear without treatment. The paediatrician will look at the baby's palate carefully to check for clefts of the soft or hard palate.

The chest

◇ Breast enlargement is seen in many infants. It is caused by stimulation of the tissue by female hormones from the placenta, and is of no significance. Sometimes the breasts produce a secretion of a milky substance due to this stimulating effect. This 'witches' milk' used to be thought to have mystical qualities.

◇ It is not generally necessary to examine the lungs with a stethoscope – a normal respiratory rate is by far the most sensitive index.

◇ Parents often notice a solid lump just below the breastbone (sternum) at the top of the abdomen (usually at 2 a.m.!). This is the xiphisternum – the extension to the sternum, made of cartilage – and is normal.

The heart

◇ The normal heart rate is usually between 100 and 140 beats per minute.

◇ The heart is also checked with a stethoscope for the sound of a murmur. Most murmurs picked up in the first few days are not dangerous. They may be due either to delay in the circulation changing from that of a foetus to that of a newborn (the patent ductus arteriousus: PDA), or to the presence of a small hole between the two main pumping chambers in the heart (ventricular septal defect: VSD). Both these problems right themselves within a few weeks or months and are harmless.

The abdomen

◇ The doctor examines the abdomen to make sure the liver, spleen and kidneys are normal, and also feels for any abnormal lumps or masses.

◇ The anus is checked to see that it's open.

◇ The umbilical cord contains three vessels (one vein and two arteries). Occasionally an umbilical hernia may be present (see 'Umbilical hernia'). This is of no significance and rarely requires surgery: it usually disappears by around the age of five.

◇ At the junction of the abdomen and the thighs, the main (femoral) arteries to the legs can be felt with the fingertips. A normal pulse will mean that there is no narrowing of the artery higher up.

The genitals

These will be inspected carefully for any abnormalities.

◇ In boys, both testes are in the scrotum. Cold hands, however, may make them disappear temporarily, as there is a reflex that pulls them up out of sight.

◇ As the testes are formed in the abdomen (near the kidneys) they have to migrate down, through the groin and into the scrotum, in the last trimester of the pregnancy. Occasionally the testes are held up on their journey. They are then termed undescended. About 3 percent of babies have this condition and 90 percent of these testes will descend on their own in the first year; the rest may require surgery after a year or so to bring one or both into the scrotum.

◇ In girls, the vulva looks rather swollen and red in comparison to later life.

◇ Occasionally the labia minora (inner lips) protrude between the labia majora (outer lips). This is common in the full-term baby and normal in even the slightly premature.

◇ Mucous tags, mucousy discharge and occasionally bleeding may be seen at the opening of the vagina. They occur because of stimulation from hormones from the placenta and are not significant.

The hips

The hip joints are examined for clicks (which are quite common, and harmless, in the newborn) or dislocation. The whole hip exam is a really important part of the examination. Your doctor will examine your baby's hips again before you and your baby are discharged from the hospital (see 'Hip issues').

The legs and feet

◇ It is normal for babies to have bow legs. The slight curvature of the tibia is caused by their posture inside the womb.

◇ Most babies hold their feet turned inwards while in the womb, and they may continue to do this for a few weeks after delivery. Occasionally this is called 'postural talipes', but it is not the talipes of club foot. If the foot can be held at right angles to the leg with the sole flat, it is a normal ankle joint. The baby will do her own exercises now that she has space, and no treatment is necessary.

◇ If there seems to be a bony block to flattening the foot, physiotherapy or splinting may be necessary.

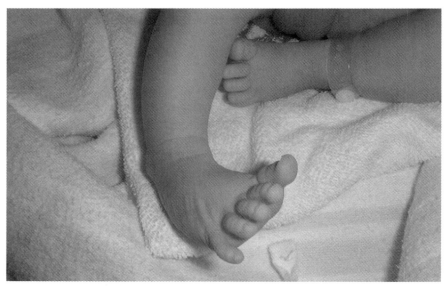

Despite its appearance, this in-turned foot is quite normal

The back

The doctor will check the spine to see that it is straight and has no faults. Very commonly there is a dimple at the base of the spine. This is quite normal and will grow out with time.

The nervous system

Throughout the examination of the nervous system, the baby's posture, muscle tone and strength, movements, responses, moods, and cry are all observed and noted.

Posture and tone

The new baby typically lies with her legs and arms flexed and tucked into her body and with her head to one side. There is not a lot of strength in her neck, but if she is placed lying on her front, she can lift her head momentarily from the bed using her 'neck extensor' muscles. These are stronger than her 'neck flexors'. If, from lying on her back, she is pulled to a sitting position, her head usually lolls back. In this position, her back is rounded. Her legs will kick alternately when she is disturbed. Her hands tend to gravitate to her mouth. Many of her movements are the result of what are termed 'primitive reflexes'.

Primitive reflexes

A baby is born with a number of automatic reactions to changes in her position or environment. These are reflexes that emanate from lower centres of consciousness in the brain. As the baby matures and develops, the higher centres take over control of her movements and these reflexes disappear. The sequence and timing of their disappearance tell us much about the neurological health of the baby.

Moro reflex

Especially obvious is her 'startle' (Moro) reflex. If the baby's chin is positioned on her chest and her head is allowed to fall back, she will respond by flinging her arms out as if to grab at something. She will then move them in an arc towards the midline of her chest. Her back may arch. At the same time she will open her eyes wide, look unhappy, and may start to cry. A test of the Moro reflex is a good check of the baby's muscle tone. To the baby's great relief, this reflex gradually disappears over the first two to three months.

Grasp

If the baby's palm is tickled, she will close her hand and try to grip the finger. Parents love it when their baby holds on to them tightly within a few minutes of being born. This reflex is so strong that the baby can actually support her body weight grasping a finger in each hand, but we don't recommend that you rely on it! Her toes will also flex in response to a similar stimulus to the sole of the foot.

Rooting

If the baby's cheek is gently brushed on one side she will turn her head in that direction. This is called the rooting reflex, and will ensure that she will root for the nipple when her cheek brushes against her mother's breast.

Walking

Holding the baby up and placing her feet on a surface will induce a crude walking movement. It is not driven from the same area as the walking later in life and this ability will disappear at a few weeks of age.

Stepping

By bringing the baby's shin in contact with the edge of a flat surface, the leg will be raised to step over it as though she were climbing a staircase.

Gallant

By holding the baby face downward over one's hand and gently scratching the skin on either side of the backbone, the baby will flex her back to the side of the scratch. It has been compared to a swimming movement, and may be a remnant of our aquatic past.

Testing the senses

After 'Is she all right?' inevitably comes 'Can she see okay?' and 'Can she hear?' In the new baby these are hard to determine except with highly technical testing. Nevertheless, a lot of relevant information can be gleaned from the clinical examination.

Sight

The baby can see, but her focal distance is short – about 17 cm. She can turn to and gaze at light, and will often stare fixedly at a face.

◇ The lenses in her eyes will be examined with an ophthalmoscope to see that they are clear and free from cataracts.

◇ The eye movements can also be tested. Holding the baby under the armpits and swinging her gently from side to side will make the eyes look in the direction of the swing. It tests the muscles that move the eyes to the outer side of the eye-socket. Sometimes the nerve that serves this muscle is stretched during delivery – this can temporarily paralyse it and give the baby a persistent squint. It usually gets better within six weeks.

Hearing

Hearing is somewhat more difficult to test clinically in the first few days, as the baby is very tolerant of loud noises. Remember, she has just emerged from the noisy environment of the womb, with her mother's aorta, the main artery of the body, banging away centimetres from her ear, the bowels gurgling and her bladder filling and emptying. She will usually respond to a clap or a loud noise if you catch her in the right mood, but this is really unreliable.

Nowadays we have proper automated testing available in many areas and it will become more and more widespread over the next few years. This testing picks up at least twice as many deaf babies as clinical methods do, and it picks them up much earlier. Hearing loss in the newborn is not rare. About 133 babies per 100,000 have a significant hearing loss that needs attention, and about half those babies have no factors in their history

that put them at risk, such as a family history of deafness or a condition that meant they spent time in a newborn intensive care unit. It is vital to spot these babies before they are six months of age so that treatment can begin and language can develop normally.

Of the two kinds of screening tests available, the easier to use and hence the most common is the 'cochlear echoes' (Transient Evoked Oto-Acoustic Emissions). The testing device sends low-intensity sounds into the ear and detects the 'clicks' evoked from the hairs in the outer hair cells of the cochlea. It is quick, reliable and easy to do, but it doesn't actually measure hearing – it does correlate well with that ability, though. The alternative method (Automatic Auditing Brainstorm Response) means placing electrodes on the baby's head to detect the response of the brainstem to auditory stimuli. It measures true hearing but is harder and more time consuming to perform. Most screening services use the first method for everyone, and then check suspect babies with the second.

Discharge examination

Just before your baby goes home your doctor will carry out a final examination. This is to check the following things:

⬦ The heart is checked to be sure that no murmurs have emerged since the first examination. Because the baby's circulation is making great changes in these first few days, some murmurs take a few days to develop.

⬦ The head circumference is re-measured now that most of the moulding has disappeared.

⬦ The umbilical cord is checked for infection, and to make sure that the normal process of drying and separation is occurring.

⬦ The baby's eyes are checked for 'stickiness', and, if necessary, tear duct massage is taught to the mother.

⬦ The skin is examined for any rashes or pimples (pustules) caused by skin infections.

⬦ The hips are rechecked, just to be on the safe side. Hips whose ligaments were marginally lax on the first day should now be much firmer in their sockets; if they are, they can be safely left alone, but will still need to be carefully followed up.

The feeding is assessed to see if it is going well. The baby is usually weighed – though at this stage whether or not there is any gain doesn't mean much.

Any questions you have can be answered. Now is the time to clear up any conflicting advice you may have been given, and to find out how to get help if things worry you after you go home. Don't waste the opportunity!

Ensure you resolve any conflicting advice you've been given

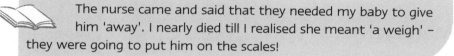

The nurse came and said that they needed my baby to give him 'away'. I nearly died till I realised she meant 'a weigh' – they were going to put him on the scales!

Small babies

Babies who weigh less than 2.5 kg ($5\frac{1}{2}$ lb) at birth are defined as small. There are several reasons why babies are small:

◇ The baby's parents may be small. In this case the baby would behave and have the same needs as any other full-term baby.
◇ The baby may be premature. Some important functions might be immature in such a baby: this could result in poor sucking and feeding, respiratory difficulty, a tendency to get cold easily or for the blood sugar level to drop, and general lethargy.
◇ The baby may be 'small for dates'. This baby is more mature than her weight implies but she is undernourished, usually because the placenta, and hence food transferral from her mother, did not function well in the final weeks.

Babies in the last two groups are given extra attention until they are stable and functioning the way a larger baby might. Obviously, if the babies are very small, unstable or require special care for any reason, they are admitted to a neonatal intensive care unit. Their management is beyond the scope of this book. However, the vast majority of babies admitted to such units do very well; if they are there because they are premature, they will generally be home by the time they are 38 weeks' gestation.

Observations

Small babies who are big enough to stay with their mother in the postnatal ward are checked regularly:

◇ respiratory rate (every four hours);
◇ heart rate (every four hours);
◇ temperature (every four hours); and
◇ heel-prick tests with Dextrostix or BM sticks to measure their blood sugar level.

Management

If the baby is a week or so premature (that is, 35 to 36 weeks' gestation) the mother can expect feeding to take a little longer to establish, because the sucking reflex may not be at full strength for a few days. It can require a lot of patience and determination to stick to breastfeeding with some of the slower ones.

In contrast, the 'small for dates' baby may have a voracious appetite and work hard to put on the weight she feels is her birthright – at her poor mother's expense. Again, patience and unlimited feeding are the go! When her weight catches up (usually within the first three months) she'll settle down to a more relaxed schedule.

It is worth remembering that these babies have poor stores of energy for the first few days. This is why an eye must be kept on their blood sugar level (by heel-prick tests) until it is stable.

These babies may also require extra feeds of formula if they are too small to wait for the arrival of the breastmilk in two to three days. In addition, their temperature must be checked regularly, because they can chill easily if they are inadequately dressed in a cool environment.

Small babies should be immunised at the usual time – from their birthday, **not** corrected for their prematurity.

The empty-handed mother

It is pretty depressing if your baby needs to be in the special care nursery instead of by your side. Quite apart from the anxiety, there is often a feeling that you have let her down because you cannot meet all her needs by yourself, and a fear that in some way your bonding with your baby will suffer (properly managed, it will not).

Special care nurseries seem to evoke different responses in different parents. Some find the technology reassuring: they feel that all the equipment is really making their baby better. Others are just terrified that their baby needs to be looked after in an environment that seems more suitable for an astronaut.

You will be encouraged to spend as much time as possible with your baby – if this feels comfortable, do it. If, on the other hand, sitting by her terrifies and panics you, don't do it. After a few days you will feel comfortable enough to stay with her for longer and longer periods. There are no hard and fast rules.

Many parents, especially mothers, go through a brief period much like grieving if their baby has a problem after birth. They grieve for the loss of the perfection they imagined during the pregnancy. They may feel disappointment and anger, as well as sadness and anxiety, as they struggle to adjust. These powerful emotions are either directed inwardly, as guilt, or outwardly, as anger towards the partner, the doctors and nurses – and even the baby.

Like every other part of the body, our mind also has to heal when it has been injured, and these emotions are a part of the healing process. Accept them for what they are – a painful but important pathway to feeling better. They will pass and, for the vast majority of mothers, be replaced by joy as the healthy baby is placed in her arms.

5

Early days

Even trained paediatricians who have babies of their own are anxious about them when they first get to the postnatal ward. Babies, for their part, sometimes aren't very reassuring either. They get mucousy, have blue spells, irregular breathing, sleep deeply or not at all and generally rarely fit into the pattern we were expecting.

After you've read this chapter, you should be able to stop worrying unnecessarily. Get some sleep if you can. You're going to need it.

Things that might worry you

There are so many little things that babies do in the early days that evoke anxiety, even panic, in new parents.

Getting through the goo

Many babies are very mucousy in the first 24 to 48 hours. They gag, and vomit clear or bloodstained (from the placenta) mucus frequently. It can be very thick, like treacle, and can cause temporary obstruction to the baby's breathing. This mucus is also the commonest cause of 'blue turns' during this period. They may struggle for breath, arching their back and terrifying the life out of the mother and nearby nurses. Everyone rushes about with medical suckers, putting the babies in the 'coma' position (though the babies are not in a coma) with warnings of choking.

Relax. Babies are born with incredibly good cough and gag reflexes. When they are just born their lungs are filled with fluid. They clear their throat and lungs and take their first breath and from then guard their airway well. They have no intention of allowing the mucus or other secretions in their throat to be inhaled. So they cough and gag and struggle to clear it before they take a breath. They manage just fine without help and would not choke even if you weren't there watching.

The mucus is produced by the stomach lining as a reaction to delivery. It may be continually produced for a day or two, so washing out the stomach with a tube does no good. The mucus sometimes also makes the baby reluctant to feed. There is no need for any special treatment, but tipping the baby onto her side and patting her back can't do any harm.

Snuffles

Attention! This is an important sentence, and will relieve much anxiety in the first few days after the baby's birth: don't worry, the baby does **not** have a cold.

Four out of five babies get fairly heavy snuffles in the first few days and weeks. When a baby feeds, the milk syphons down her throat and up into the back of her nose, and the delicate lining of the nose produces lots of extra mucus to protect itself. If the baby regurgitates or vomits, stomach juice, which is acid, ends up in

In the first few days after birth, baby does *not* have a cold

the nose as well. After a few weeks this is usually much worse at night, because the baby sleeps for longer periods undisturbed then (we hope!), and the mucus just accumulates.

If the snuffles are interfering with your baby's sleeping or feeding, local decongestant or plain saline nasal drops might help, but your baby will hate it. You will therefore end up chasing a moving target – and the nose is a pretty small target!

My advice is to ignore the snuffles; they will go away.

Cough

Occasionally, the amount of mucus produced by the nose can be so great that it pours out the back of the nose and down into the throat (pharynx), where it collects and gives the baby a 'rattly chest' or a cough. Again, this is usually nothing to worry about.

If your baby really catches a cold or some other viral infection she is unlikely to have only snuffles and a cough. She will probably have a raised temperature and will appear unwell. Also, the infected cough is more likely to be repetitive (multiple coughs per episode) and productive (of mucus), like a smoker's cough, or barking in character. You will also know that your baby is just not herself, in which case hotfoot it to the doctor.

Sticky eyes

About 15 percent of babies develop sticky eyes within a few days of birth. One or both eyes start to discharge mucus or pus from under the lids. It can gum the lids together, especially after the baby has been asleep for a while.

What the baby has is a blocked tear duct. Only rarely is it conjunctivitis – ninety-nine times out of a hundred she does not have a contagious infection that can be passed to the other eye or to you. And her sight will not be affected.

If you look at the inner corner of your eye, you will see a fleshy bead-shaped structure. This is the tear sac, which collects the tears secreted by the eye, and passes them down a narrow tube (the tear duct) to the cavity of your nose. That's why your nose runs when you cry.

In babies there is a tendency for the bottom end of this duct to become blocked with a little plug of mucus. There is then a nice warm test tube of tears that incubates and grows whatever germs happen to be around at the time, and this produces the pus. The problem will disappear when the plug at the bottom of the tube is cleared – which is done by the body's normal processes – but until then it requires a little treatment:

◇ Pressing gently with your fingertip from inner corner of the eye to halfway down the side of the nose will squeeze out fluid and pus from both ends of the tear duct. Do this for three strokes three times a day. Then clean the eye – with saline, ideally, but cooled, boiled water will do.

◇ If the eye becomes very gummy, it is often helpful to then instil some antibiotic eyedrops (these can be prescribed by your doctor). This does not cure the condition, but it does tend to cut down the number of germs within the tear duct and stop dried pus making the mucus plug even more difficult for the body to remove.

◇ The tear duct massage should be continued until the eye has been clear for a few days. It is unusual for the problem to last for more than a few days; if it does, the treatment is just the same. You should only consider getting an ophthalmologist to probe the duct if the stickiness and weeping of the eye continue for nine months. Even then, delaying the probing usually results in the duct clearing itself spontaneously.

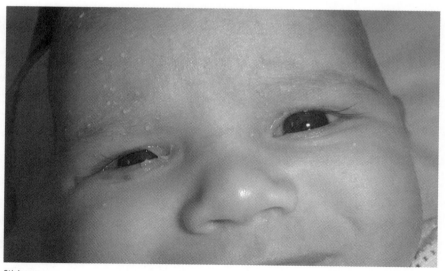

Sticky eye

Hiccups

You probably noticed that your baby was hiccupping in the womb, and now she hiccups outside. It tends to occur during or after feeds, and these enormous hiccups rack her little body like convulsions! Don't worry. It is a sign of gratitude for a good feed – no treatment is necessary.

Fever on day two

Many babies have a little fever on day two or day three. This does not represent infection or any problem. It usually coincides with the baby being at her driest, that is, after she has lost the extra water in her body and before the milk has come in.

At this age babies are very susceptible to overwrapping. So make sure, if the weather is warm, that she does not have too much covering her. As a rule, babies should be dressed in the same number of layers and thickness of clothing as you are. Babies do not need especially warm clothes unless conditions are very cool.

The problem with babies' temperature control is not that they need more insulation than older people, but that they cannot compensate for rapid changes. If we are outside in thin clothes and a cold change comes through, our bodies compensate for that by shivering and closing down our skin blood flow, retaining warmth in the core of our bodies; small babies are not able to compensate as efficiently. So dress the baby appropriately for the current environment, and if the temperature changes, respond accordingly.

Be very careful about exposing your baby to direct sunlight, especially within the first week of life. Their bodies are relatively fluid-deficient at this time, so direct sunlight can cause a rapid rise in body temperature, which can be very harmful. Avoid sun kicks until she is a few weeks older – and even then, it is wise to take special care.

Weight loss

When babies are in the womb they are, in effect, marine animals, floating in a primordial sea. When they are born, their bodies are relatively waterlogged and they need to get rid of all that extra water. Nature has arranged this in a very clever way. Firstly, your milk does not come in for a couple of days, so the baby does not drink very much, just a dribble of colostrum per feed. This allows her to get rid of her extra water. Secondly, she continues to pass urine and therefore loses weight. This is absolutely normal. Many babies will lose up to 10 percent of their body weight (that is, 350 g or 12 oz in a normal-sized baby). This is another reason babies are relatively uninterested in feeding in the first couple of days. Nature tells them that it's not necessary.

Skin rash: toxic erythema

'I think there must be fleas in this hospital – my baby's covered with bites!'

A day or so after delivery it is common for a baby to suddenly come out in a skin rash that makes her look as if she has been attacked by fleas or mosquitoes. The rash has a yellowish head with a surrounding wide red area. Occasionally there may be many such spots, which all run together, making the baby look as if she has the measles. This rash is called 'toxic erythema' – it is completely harmless and not the least toxic!

It seems to relate to the baby's skin first coming in contact with clothes, especially cotton. It does not mean the baby is allergic to anything or that she has particularly sensitive skin. The rash does not cause discomfort and will go away after a few days.

Dry skin

Most babies born at full term, and all babies born post-term, develop dry skin in the days after delivery. At its most obvious, the skin can have deep cracks and fissures and the baby may peel off sheets of dead skin like a snake. More usually, though, the skin just gently scales, especially over the hands and feet.

The top layer of skin that has been in contact with the amniotic fluid is merely being replaced. It doesn't mean the baby will have a permanently dry skin. It has no relationship to eczema and it needs no treatment.

However, moisturising – with sorbolene, for example – will make the baby's skin look a little more like the proverbial baby's bottom, at least for twenty minutes!

Fat necrosis

Some babies develop rubbery lumps under the skin after a few days, usually along the line of the jaw or the cheekbone. This is due to the fat cells in the skin rupturing during delivery. This releases fat into the tissue under the skin, which sets up an inflammatory reaction. It's quite harmless – the lumps will disappear in a few weeks.

Sweating

It is not uncommon for babies to sweat profusely from their head or their feet, enough to wet the bedclothes. The cause is unknown, but the sweating creates no problem and is not associated with any disease.

Blue around the mouth

There is an amazing old wives' tale linking blue colouration around the baby's mouth with colic. Don't ask me what the connection is – there is none. This colouration probably relates to congestion of the veins after a vigorous bout of sucking, and is of no significance at all.

Nails

Most parents are in awe of the perfection in their baby's hands and feet at birth. The nails are a bit of an issue for them, though, as the fingernails are often long at birth and the baby rakes them across her cheek, causing scratch marks, just before the grandparents visit. Read on.

Long fingernails

Full-term and post-term babies are frequently born with long fingernails. By coincidence, babies tend to hold their arms fully flexed at the elbow, which puts the sharp nails right up against their cheeks. Babies' cheeks are not meant to look lacerated, so mothers usually want to cut the nails. For the first couple of weeks it is probably better to put cloth mittens on your baby's hands than to cut the nails. Attempting to trim soft, almost transparent, fingernails can be difficult – it is very easy to cut into the nail bed and draw blood.

Later, it is probably better to use clippers rather than scissors – and go very carefully, because it is easy to cut the nails too short. I have trouble supporting the mothercraft idea of biting your baby's nails, as it is hard to do and harder to be accurate. A good time to cut them is during feeds, when your baby is so busy that she tends to keep her hands still.

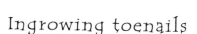

Ingrowing toenails

Many babies are born with very short toenails, especially on the big toes. The nails are quite normal, and grow out without problems. Occasionally, as the nails grow, the skin against the nail's leading edge becomes red and inflamed. All that is required is a little local antiseptic for a week or so. Even if the skin starts developing crusty granulations it still requires no further treatment. Only the most severe cases need antibiotics or referral to a surgeon.

Infected nails

It is not unusual for the edges of babies' fingernails to become red and inflamed after the first few days. The official name of the condition is paronychia. It usually starts where the corner of the nail meets the skin, often with a little of the cuticle flaking off. In the early stages local antiseptic is all that is required, but if the infection starts to spread towards the joint of the finger, antibiotics are usually necessary.

Pink-stained nappies

Sometimes mothers get a fright in the first few days. When they change their baby's nappy the urine appears to be bloodstained! In fact it is not blood – it is a pinkish-staining chemical called 'urate', which the babies pass in high concentration for the first few days after delivery. It is quite normal.

Little girls sometimes do have bloodstained nappies. A proportion of baby girls actually menstruate following the withdrawal of the hormones they had from the placenta. If they don't actually produce blood, most of them will produce a vaginal discharge in the first few days. This is quite normal. Many girls will also have a mucus tag hanging from the back of the vagina. This is also caused by hormones from the placenta; it disappears after a few days or weeks.

Urinary stream

While we are on the subject of nappies, most little boys show their respect for their mother at an early stage by weeing over her. This shower offers you a chance to make a worthwhile observation! It means the baby's urinary stream is perfectly normal. If the urine just dribbles out of the little boy, it is a good idea to let your paediatrician or midwife know.

Occasionally boy babies can have flaps in their urinary passage from the bladder, which prevent a good stream and can cause problems if left untreated. This problem does not occur in little girls.

Tongue-tie

There is commonly a thin membrane on the underside of the tongue that connects it to the floor of the mouth. This is a normal structure called the frenulum. Occasionally it can extend far forward, nearly to the tip of the tongue. This is called tongue-tie. Rumours circulate that if the membrane extends far forward, it needs to be surgically incised. This is incorrect. As the tongue grows, the membrane will retreat to its more normal position. While it still extends to the front of the tongue, it usually causes no problem with feeding or crying, and should be left alone.

Very occasionally the membrane is thick and fleshy and may restrict movement of the tongue so much that the baby cannot extend her tongue forward beyond her gum. This might mean she can't latch on to the breast properly, and breastfeeding is painful for mother and disappointing for baby. This condition is called 'ankyloglossia', and under these circumstances surgery might be necessary.

Umbilical cleaning

The umbilical cord is usually not the mother's favourite part of her baby. Most will touch it only reluctantly, and fear that any handling will cause it to start bleeding or hurt the baby in some way.

The facts are that the cord has no nerve fibres, so handling it can't cause the baby pain (cutting the cord didn't hurt the baby either). Within an hour of delivery, the arteries are in spasm, so bleeding is most unlikely. As long as the cord remains uninfected, important bleeding is impossible after the first day. Spots of blood from the cord are from the clots within it, and are not a problem. The cord is very tough.

The cord should be cleaned at regular intervals because germs grow readily on its surface, and especially in the gutter between the cord and the skin. If you are in a room where there are other babies, use diluted methylated spirits to clean it. If you are in a single room, water is usually all that is necessary. The methylated spirits cuts down the possibility of cross-infection between babies as the cord is a common source of germs; if you are in a room on your own the germs are just from you, so there's no danger to anyone.

Clean the base of the cord, and at the same time gently pull on the cord to get down into the gutter. If your baby cries while this is being done, it is not because it is painful, but because the methylated spirits or water is cold to her skin.

If the cord gets smelly, clean it more frequently. If the skin around the umbilicus becomes red, it may be developing an infection, so tell your paediatrician or midwife.

Once you get home you can stop using the methylated spirits as there is then no danger of cross-infection. Just clean the cord with a dry cotton bud and it should fall off soon after. Cords can last from four days to six weeks.

Umbilical granuloma

Sometimes after the cord falls off you might notice a wet, pinkish knob of tissue on the leftover stump. No matter how hard you clean it, it keeps weeping fluid and won't heal over. This can last for weeks. Sometimes the lump even gets bigger. It is called a granuloma and is due to the healing (granulation) tissue getting too enthusiastic and not allowing the normal skin to cover it.

If you take your baby to your health nurse or doctor they will put on a little copper sulphate, and it will rapidly disappear.

Umbilical hernia

Some babies develop a swelling under the umbilicus that gets larger when they yell or tense up their tummy. If you squeeze it, it may gurgle, and the contents may disappear back into the abdomen. This is the one hernia in the body that you can completely ignore. It never causes problems, doesn't ever burst, never strangulates and doesn't require surgery.

It is just the small gap in the muscle layer of the abdominal wall through which the umbilical vessels to the placenta passed, and is composed of a very strong membrane. It will disappear gradually – in the vast majority of babies it is completely gone before the child reaches the age of five, and usually it's gone long before that.

Unsettled sleep behaviour

This sentence is worth remembering: anything that reminds your baby of being in the womb will tend to comfort and settle her.

> Anything that reminds your baby of being in the womb will help comfort and settle her.

Appreciate what changes a new baby has gone through! From the warmth and muffled security of the womb she has now moved into a cool, noisy world, plus she's in a strange cot and has a nappy on. Some babies make the transition smoothly, but others are a bit more nostalgic and react accordingly.

If your baby is unsettled in these early days, try to appreciate what she feels. Anything that reminds her of being in the womb will tend to comfort and settle her. Hold her against your chest with her ear against your heartbeat. Wrap her up so she feels contained and secure. Put her against you, skin to skin, with a cover over both of you. And, of course, feed her if you think she wants to suck (you cannot overfeed her at this time).

When she feels your skin in contact with hers, and hears the familiar sound of your heartbeat, the sound that filled her world when she was inside you, she will settle.

Wrapping babies

Wrapping your baby snuggly, with a rounded back and contained limbs, can help her get to sleep – it reminds her of being in the womb and suppresses the startle reflex.

Most babies prefer to be wrapped snuggly to settle, at least until the startle reflex disappears, at about three months. As described elsewhere, this reflex is upsetting for babies. When the head falls backwards, the arms fling out in a primitive attempt to grasp and hold onto something. Like the sensation of falling, this whole involuntary sequence gives them a fright. Loud noises or other stimuli can also bring on the reflex. Wrapping babies suppresses it, which means they find it easier to settle themselves.

Dummies and thumb-sucking

If a baby wants to suck, she should be allowed to do so. If you don't give her a dummy, she will probably find her fingers or her thumb. In fact a recent study showed that about a third of two-and-a-half-year-olds sucked fingers or thumbs and another third used dummies. All the bad reports about dummies are suspect. However, a 'dormal' (a miniature bottle filled with sugary drink) dissolves teeth and should never be used. The thumb is probably more convenient than the dummy, as it tends not to fall on the floor out of reach. Some parents reject dummies because of their appearance, others prefer their babies to have a dummy because at some

Wrapping your baby

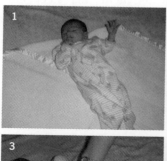

1 Turn over the corner of the blanket and put the baby down with his head over the folded edge

2 Wrap his arm using the edge of the blanket

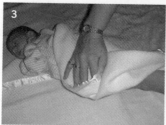

3 Put the fold behind him to capture his arm

4 Roll his body to secure the blanket

5 Repeat with his other arm holding blanket against his chest

6 Hold tail of blanket and roll baby over to secure

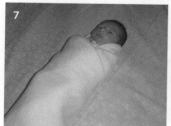

7 Our little babushka, wrapped up snugly

8 Take the long tail of the blanket and pull it up and over ...

9 ... to around his back and tuck behind his shoulder. He's now secure and stable.

time in the future it can be thrown away. The baby is sucking her thumb or dummy for very good reasons – it calms her, helps her sleep and comforts her. Her parents' opinion of the aesthetic aspects don't interest her, and they should mind their own business.

Dummies don't cause disease and sucking her thumb won't make her teeth stick out and cost you a fortune in orthodontics. Neither will her thumb shrink. For everyone's peace of mind, allow your baby to make up her mind about whether or not she wishes to suck and, if so, what.

Fourth-day blues

The fourth day is a bitch. Your milk has just come in and you have these two beach balls on your chest. Your baby is slightly jaundiced and you don't know what is going on with her. She has been feeding two-hourly for the last 24 hours and you can't remember ever feeling so tired before. The newness and delight of the birth are starting to fade and you feel just plain depressed. Everyone who comes to see you looks only at the baby and tells you how wonderful you must be feeling. Your bottom is sore and you can't sit comfortably, or if you had a Caesarean, your incision hurts. On top of that, opening your bowels is difficult and very painful.

Many of the problems with the baby seem to explode out of all proportion today. She seems to have an insurmountable feeding problem. You suspect her jaundice is not the normal type but some new disease. When she cries, she seems to be blaming you for being born and you are sure all the doctors and nurses think you're a lot of trouble. The fact that your common sense tells you that all this is untrue is not much help.

The only comforting thing to say about this picture of woe is that most mothers go through it and the feelings will soon pass. They seem to be related to the withdrawal of the high levels of placenta hormones that were, believe it or not, putting you on a 'high' during your pregnancy. Day four seems to bring all these things to a head. My recommendation is to find a quiet corner (the shower is a popular choice) and have a good cry.

Sometimes this depression can last several days or even longer, but that is unusual (see 'Postnatal depression'). If it seems to be happening to you, do not keep it to yourself. It is important, it will be taken seriously, and it can be treated. It is also probably more common than women let on.

When I was pregnant, if I rode in a bus and it went over a bump I would always put a hand on my tummy to protect my baby. After the birth I missed her in there. Once the bus went over a bump and I put my hand to my tummy and felt a rush of grief and loss that she wasn't there any more.

Naming the baby

After a few years in this game I now realise that there is no way I ought to write this section! Naming babies is a deeply personal process and often bears little relationship to logic, aesthetics, common sense or foresight. People can get very fond of the weirdest names, and I have now learned not to throw back my head and roar with laughter when I am told that a baby is going to be called Crudidge or Waffinberry. However, against my better judgement, I would like to impart a few little rules that have come my way:

◇ Remember that your baby has to live with this name for the rest of his or her life. Within a short time she will even start to look like her name. So give her a name to be proud of, not a name to please a rich aunt, or to follow a family tradition, or because your favourite football team won the cup.

◇ If you give her name a strange spelling, she will have a lifetime of spelling it out for others. I think it is a real problem to use a common name with an uncommon spelling. So if you want to call your daughter Alison, don't spell it Allysoine.

◇ Cadence and rhythm are very important. Try the name out with the surname and see if it is easy to say and has a nice sound. Dalton Hilton just doesn't work.

◇ Be careful of initials. Avoid WC, VD, STD (think of all the telephone jokes …), BUM, and more subtly, even RC.

◇ Humour is okay, but make sure the joke is going to last more than a few months. I once had a patient who was a 700 g (25 oz) premature baby. The parents called him Goliath, for a laugh. I don't know if the little lad appreciated it when he was fourteen years old.

⋄ Try to avoid fashion. Some babies who were born in the 1960s are probably now pretty sick of their names, especially Freelove Jones or Moonglow Smith. Also, if you're the fifteenth John in your class at school it can be a pain, so check the papers for the latest common names and avoid them.

⋄ Some people have to use family names. However, why not make that their second name and make their first name a nice one?

⋄ Don't feel pressured to name your baby in the first few days. if you need time, take it. Also, don't feel embarrassed about changing your mind a few days (or weeks) down the road. It's an important issue.

When it comes to conflict about the name between parents, an obstetrics friend of mine has a great system that he recommends. The parents go into separate rooms and write a list of their ten favourite names, scoring each one out of ten in preference order. They then swap lists and delete all those names they hate. They then score the others out of ten. Usually there are a couple of names that both parents give seven or eight to – they can then work on them without wasting time on names that have no chance of getting up. In the event of a tie, they toss a coin for it or fight!

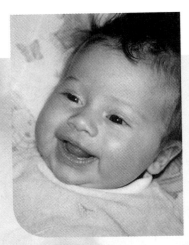

6

Important medical matters

T hese are all fairly technical things, but they are important and common enough to need explanation.

The Newborn Screening Test

The Newborn Screening Test is a blood test performed on your baby in the first week after birth, usually about day four. Every baby in the country gets one. A blood sample is taken by a heel prick; the blood is absorbed onto a special piece of blotting paper. The sample is dried and sent to a laboratory for testing. This test is designed to find those very few babies who have some rare diseases called 'inborn errors of metabolism'. That is, they are born missing some functions concerned with the breakdown of food into the building blocks of the body and/or the building up of body tissues from those building blocks. These disorders are extremely rare (one in 10,000–100,000).

The Newborn Screening Test these days incorporates two other important tests:

◇ One tests the thyroid function and will pick up if your baby's thyroid is not producing enough hormone (this is an important cause of brain damage if it is not picked up immediately).
◇ The other tests for cystic fibrosis. This is a disease of the excreting glands of the body that has important effects on the baby's lungs and digestive system.

You are not informed if there is no problem detected by the test. However, it is not unusual for the laboratory to ask for a further sample in the case of a borderline result or laboratory problems. Under these circumstances, the test will almost always be negative (that is, no problem is found) and the laboratory will inform you of this result as soon as the test is done.

If the result happens to be positive you will hear about it within a few days of the test.

Hip issues

Paediatricians are obsessed with hips. Don't misunderstand me: our concern is that the hip joints of newborns develop properly, so that the ball and socket joint has a deep, stable socket that will take the weight of the body while walking through life.

At birth the socket is not fully developed, the bones around it are made of soft cartilage and the ligaments supporting it are relatively lax. In order to develop a stable socket, a process that takes about a year, the head of the leg bone (femur) needs to press gently but firmly against the centre of the cavity of the socket. Over the months this deepens the socket, and then when it turns to bone it is the right depth and shape.

If the socket is shallow at birth, or the ligaments are too loose, the pressure from the head of the femur might not be firm enough and the socket may not deepen. The result can be a hip that dislocates when weight is put on it when the baby finally walks.

This condition is preventable if we can find all those loose or shallow-socketed hips and treat them before the joint turns to bone.

Unfortunately, it isn't simple. One of the many functions of the female hormones produced by mother's placenta is to soften her ligaments to make the birth of the baby easier. These hormones cross the placenta and have a similar effect on the newborn baby. Consequently, most newborns are 'double-jointed' and their hip joints have a fair amount of give between the ball and the socket. This is normal.

When the hip joints are examined after birth, backwards pressure is exerted on the leg with the hips bent at right angles to the body. This pressure can cause the head of the leg bone (femur) to move a little within the pelvic socket. These babies are said to have 'clicky hips'. Usually this looseness diminishes and then disappears over the first days and weeks.

Far less commonly (about one to two babies per 1000), the hip joint of the baby can be dislocated out of the joint, so called 'congenital dislocation'.

We used to call this whole condition 'Congenital Dislocation of the Hip' (CDH), but it is now clear that some babies develop a shallow socket for genetic reasons, without ever having looseness of the hip joint, so we now call it 'Developmental Dysplasia of the Hip' (DDH). Dysplasia means 'poor formation'.

We know that certain groups of babies are more at risk from this condition than others. These are:

◇ those with a family history of CDH/DDH
◇ babies who had breech births
◇ babies who had only a small amount of amniotic fluid
◇ babies who have other evidence of a cramped environment in the uteru;
◇ babies who are found to have dislocatable hips on examination following birth
◇ first-born babies
◇ females.

These factors are cumulative. For instance, if your baby is a girl, firstborn and a breech delivery, the chance of needing treatment for DDH becomes as high as one in fifteen.

The clinical examination of the baby's hips should always be done by someone skilled at detecting DDH. As already mentioned, it involves holding the hip firmly at right angles to the axis of the body with the baby on his back facing the examiner who then gently attempts to push the ball of the femur backwards out of the socket. Having done that, the leg is then rotated outwards, so that the baby is in a 'frog' posture. This tests the stability of the joint to dislocation.

Any baby who has a suspicious examination or who is in a sufficiently high-risk group should be investigated with an ultrasound of the hip joints. This is usually done at the age of about a month, unless the joint is very loose, in which case it is done immediately. Waiting a month gives the lax ligaments a little time to tighten up after the placental hormone influence is removed.

X-rays can be done as well from the age of four to five months (when there's more bone in the joint). X-rays remain the 'gold standard' diagnostic tool for excluding DDH.

Treatment

If the head of the femur can be persuaded to leave the socket or there is excess 'give' in the joint, most paediatricians and orthopaedic specialists prescribe a 'Pavlik harness'. This is a device made of straps and Velcro, and it holds the hips up at right angles to the axis of the body. This increases the pressure of the head of the femur on the socket and causes the socket to deepen.

> The harness is a bit of a nuisance, but nothing more

We no longer use 'double nappies' to do this job. They double the laundry and don't work. Also, they pull the legs out into the 'frog' position, which is unnecessary and can be harmful. The Pavlik harness just stops the baby stretching his legs out (which rotates the head of the femur to the back of the socket). He remains free to move his knees apart or almost together. The harness is a bit of a nuisance, but that's all.

It is usually all right to bathe your baby a couple of times a week without the harness, but the rest of the time the harness should be worn. Occasionally your doctor may not even allow removal during bathing – you should ask. After a short time, though, you'll all get used to it, and usually it'll only be on for about twelve weeks. When it comes off, your baby's hips will be normal for the rest of his life – so it's worth it.

Another way to check your baby's hips

In the first few months, there is another useful physical sign of the possibility of DDH. When your baby is lying on his back on the change table, normally the hips can be spread apart so that his knees can touch the surface of the table (or nearly touch). If it feels as if there is a block to that movement, get your paediatrician to examine your baby's hips, just to be on the safe side.

Jaundice

Usually on the second or third day, most babies' skin starts to go a little yellow in colour. This is jaundice. As the days pass, this colour may deepen, and the whites of the eyes may also become yellow.

The jaundice of infancy has no relationship to the jaundice in older children and adults, which is associated with illnesses, especially of the liver. The baby's jaundice is just part of the baby adapting to life outside his mother's womb.

The cause

Jaundice is caused by a substance called bilirubin, which is the breakdown product of haemoglobin, the red pigment in blood. Every day, 1 percent of the red blood cells in the body are being broken down, producing bilirubin. While the baby is in the womb this bilirubin is passed across the placenta and processed by the mother's liver so that it can be excreted. The foetus's liver needs to do very little of this work. Once the baby has been born, however, his liver has to learn how to process the bilirubin for itself. This takes a few days, so during those few days the jaundice level of the baby will rise steadily. In most babies it never rises to a high level and nothing needs to be done about it. He just gets a great tan.

However, in some babies the level may continue to rise, till it is higher than average. In **very** high quantities, circulating bilirubin can be dangerous to a baby. It is therefore a good idea to make sure that the jaundice reaches nowhere near such levels.

Testing

◇ Your doctor can estimate the jaundice level by pressing the baby's nose and observing the colour of the skin, and by noting how far the jaundice colour extends down the baby's body.

◇ Some hospitals now monitor the jaundice level using devices that flash a standard dose of light against the baby's skin. The jaundice pigment in the skin absorbs the blue colour in the light and the device measures the amount of light absorbed to estimate the level of jaundice.

◇ If the jaundice levels are higher than average, the bilirubin level will be measured and checked, using blood tests, once or twice a day. In addition, other blood tests may be ordered to check for other conditions that increase the rate of red blood cell breakdown in the body, such as incompatibility between the baby's and the mother's blood groups.

If the level is found to be rising quickly, or rising to moderate levels, your doctor will start treatment. Remember, though, that the safety margin is very large – while the baby is under such care, there is no danger to his health.

Treatment

The level of jaundice in the baby can be controlled using phototherapy. This is a simple procedure – the naked baby is exposed to ordinary fluorescent light. The bilirubin absorbs the energy from the light (actually the visible blue part of the spectrum) and this energy breaks the bilirubin down so that it can be easily excreted. We use phototherapy as a holding measure until the baby's liver is able to handle the bilirubin for itself.

While the baby is under phototherapy, pads are put over his eyes – they stop him being dazzled and help him sleep.

When the baby first goes under the lights, his temperature will be taken every now and then, to make sure he doesn't get cold. He is fed as normal. Some jaundiced babies, however, are a bit sleepy, and are rather lazy on the breast. If this is the case, it may be a good idea to express your milk and give it to the baby in a bottle, or (but this unusual) to give the baby some formula if feeding is not established. Once the baby's jaundice level starts to come down, he usually wakes promptly and feeds much better, so extra feeds can then be stopped.

As the jaundice is broken down by the light, the breakdown products are passed out in the stool. These tend to make the stool rather more loose and frequent than before. Also, it may become more greenish in colour. These changes merely demonstrate that the phototherapy is doing its job and the bilirubin is being more efficiently eliminated from the body.

A few babies (not being used to sunbathing!) cry for the first few hours under the lights. This phase quickly passes, though, as the baby adjusts to his new circumstances and starts to enjoy basking in the light.

Prolonged jaundice

The jaundice level starts to come down from about day five onwards, with or without the help of the lights. It then usually drops rapidly over the next few days. Unless it looks as if it's increasing (a rare happening), it should be ignored.

However, it is not unusual for the jaundice, though paler, to remain for some weeks. Babies in whom this occurs are almost invariably breastfed. It seems that some substance in the milk stops the baby's liver completely eliminating the bilirubin. The slight remaining jaundice never does any harm at all, and if you wait it will slowly fade and disappear.

If you're tired of your friends' 'amusing' references to the little lemon, though, try stopping breastfeeding for 48 hours. During this time, feed the baby formula and express your breasts to keep up your milk flow. (Freeze the milk for the babysitter to use later.) This might speed up the disappearance of the jaundice, but it doesn't always.

Breastfeeding

We've come a long way since 'Breast is best'. For today's woman, a better slogan would perhaps be: 'Breastfeeding is normal!' The last thing a busy mother needs is to think that breastfeeding is an added 'extra', a kind of gift that only highly dedicated women bestow on their babies. We know that biologically it is run of the mill; everyone hanging off our branch of the tree of life does it, because it's normal and appropriate.

The issue nowadays is, how do you get a new mother to understand that her body is designed for feeding, and how do you give her the confidence to do it? The art of breastfeeding is truly a 'confidence trick'. We know that the women who do it well and easily are the ones who never consider that they won't be able to. These women are surrounded by helpers who teach them how to attach the baby to the breast properly, and always give them the impression that it will work.

The problem starts with the dreaded 'complementary' bottle feed on day three, and the other 'helpful' people, the ones who suggest that it's all very hard, and painful, and difficult, and 'you're a bit tired, so you sleep tonight and I'll give the baby a bottle of formula'. They are, I'm sure, very kind, but they are sabotaging the whole process. They are breastfeeding's subtle enemy.

Studies of new mothers have shown that even teaching them how to mix formula before they go home from hospital reduces the number of successful breastfeeders significantly. It sends a quiet signal to these anxious women that their breastfeeding might fail. For a new mother, with her apparently vulnerable, totally reliant baby, breastfeeding is a big responsibility. Neither the breast nor the baby tells them how much milk is getting in. They just have to assume it's enough.

There is little else like this in the world any more. Normally we can check the data or get advice or think it through … But this is just the breast and the baby, doing their own thing.

Giving and receiving

As well as giving the best nutrition that money can't buy, by breastfeeding we are also giving (and receiving) much more. The whole process is loaded with communication – the mother and baby alone together in a bubble of warmth, smell, touch, gaze, and love; open channels to each other. When mothers breastfeed, both they and the baby secrete comfort hormones called endorphins (morphine-like substances that the body produces) which soothe and calm. Not surprisingly, breastfeeding has been called addictive. It's designed that way. Like sex, it's another part of the reproductive process that nature persuades us to do and enjoy.

We probably don't fully appreciate many of the advantages of breastfeeding to our babies. There are substances in the milk whose reason for being there is completely unknown – so far! – but you can bet they have a useful function.

There are also many advantages that we **do** appreciate. In Part III, we discuss how breastfeeding grows the best brains around, and the delicious variation of different tastes that the breastfed baby experiences. And it's cheap, easily transportable, and doesn't need sterilising. It's perfect for your baby in every way.

Breastfeeding also virtually immunises against bacterial gastroenteritis and there is a lower incidence of respiratory tract and middle ear infections – this lasts for years – in children who were breastfed.

Getting started with breastfeeding is not always easy. It seems strange, but in primates (that is, higher mammals such as apes) the ability to breastfeed is not fully instinctive – a little teaching can be helpful. In chimpanzee troupes, older females teach the younger ones how to do it. This means that getting gorillas in zoos to breastfeed has been difficult – there are usually only a few in any zoo, so when a gorilla has a baby there is usually no experienced female to teach her how to feed the little one. To overcome this, zoos have tried allowing the gorilla to watch humans breastfeed, or playing them videotapes of gorillas feeding their young.

Maternity hospitals have lots of experienced staff to help you get started – make sure you make use of this vital resource. Ask for help, especially with the early feeds.

> Maternity hospitals have experienced staff to help you get started. Make use of this vital resource, especially with the early feeds.

The first few days

Many babies are sleepy in the first two or three days, and not wildly enthusiastic about feeding. This is not really surprising, as there is no more than a dribble of colostrum for them when they wake, and being sensible people, babies do only what is rewarding. Take the opportunity to get some rest – when your milk comes in, a little light will come on in your baby's head and your life will not be the same again!

Colostrum

Sometime before you have your baby, and in increasing quantities after, the breast produces colostrum. This is a clear to yellow-coloured fluid that is full of antibodies and immunity-promoting cells. These substances line the baby's bowel and set up the start of immunity against gastroenteritis. The average breast produces about 2–12 ml of colostrum per feed. Not a big meal, but enough. It is certainly good for the baby, but it is not too much of a problem if the baby misses out on it for any reason. The baby's bowel will catch up when the breastmilk is available, and breastmilk contains all the same substances, just with lactose (sugar) added.

Water feeds

Babies are relatively waterlogged when they are born. The gap of two to three days before the milk comes in is designed to allow them to get rid of this extra water. It is most unusual for your baby to become dehydrated, so he should not be offered water feeds. There is never a need for glucose and water; this will just make your baby vomit and will offer her very little nourishment. He will come to no harm if you both patiently await the arrival of your breastmilk.

Milk 'coming in'

At about two and a half days the milk 'comes in', and you will feel a change in your breasts – they will feel firmer and warmer. About twelve hours after that sensation starts the milk starts to flow. Just before that, and for the next day or two, your baby will demand to be fed much more often – sometimes every one or two hours (the 'feeding frenzy') – as he instinctively maximises your milk flow. This can really wear you out, but have no fear. Your baby will settle down as he induces a good supply, then he will feed for longer periods of time, less frequently.

During this time especially you *cannot* overfeed your baby. Now is not the time to worry about regular spaced feeds, the baby sleeping, the baby having tummy ache, the baby being too demanding or how you'll cope if he keeps feeding like this! He won't. Just hang in there and he will fall into a more tolerable pattern.

Attaching the baby to the breast

This is the main technique that you and your baby have to learn. Some babies, if they're allowed to, will suck on the nipple as if it is a bottle teat. This is not a rewarding technique, because it produces no colostrum for the baby and soreness (and even blistering) of the nipple for you. Getting your baby attached properly is critical to breastfeeding, so get the best help you can for these early feeds.

Your baby should be presented with the breast before he is howling and tense, ideally, so you and he are both as relaxed as possible. Make sure you are comfortable, sitting or lying on your side. Unwrap the baby so that you can both enjoy the skin contact – if it's a cool day put a blanket over both of you. Gently talk to him and let his lips stroke your nipple. Try to avoid putting a hand on the back of his neck – this makes him withdraw and raise his tongue. He should respond by opening his mouth wide and 'rooting' for the nipple. The idea then is to get the whole of the nipple and some breast into his mouth so he can hold it by suction up against the back of his palate. This will draw much of the areola (the pigmented area around the nipple) into his mouth – there may be only a rim of it outside his mouth above and none below. This immobilises the breast and allows him to squeeze the milk ducts that lie under the areola. He does this by:

◇ jaw action on the areola: you can see the muscles right out to his ears move as he does it. If he sucks in his cheeks, he's not on properly;
◇ a rolling action with his tongue, from the front of his mouth to the back, so he milks the breast like a paint-roller.

Once the flow has started and there is an unbroken column of milk down his throat, the milk will 'siphon' out of the breast.

Both these actions cause the colostrum or milk to squirt out of the breast into his throat to be swallowed. The process usually has some help from the 'letdown' reflex.

The nipple is only used to immobilise the breast in the mouth. There is no rubbing of the skin and no reason for soreness to develop if the attachment is right. After a feed check the nipple: there should be no distortion of its shape. If it looks squashed or out of shape you probably need to improve the attachment of the baby to your breast.

Positioning the baby

◇ Make sure you are both comfortable and relaxed.
◇ Let the breast fall into the baby's mouth, then bring the baby to the breast; don't put the breast in the baby's mouth.
◇ The baby's head shouldn't be too flexed or extended – you try swallowing with your neck stretched or scrunched up!

Positioning baby for breastfeeding

1 Baby gazing at mother, mouth opening as breast approaches. Note: no hand on the back of baby's head.

2 Lining up nipple to nose. Nice head extension (chin up) – chin will come into the breast well. The start of a good gape.

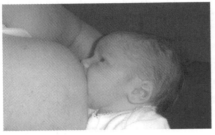

3 If breast is large, pinch to guide nipple to mouth. Note fingers on same plane as baby's lips.

4 Baby on. Mouth clear and open – nice gape.

5 Shows nice carrying position for a relaxing feed, head supported by forearm (not in crook of elbow). Mother's shoulders are relaxed, not hunched or rotated forward.

6 Contented, tranquillised baby (and mother) after feed.

7 Small babies manage well, too! Nice gape, clear nostrils.

◇ If you are having to press the breast to avoid it obstructing his nose, change his position so the nipple points more towards the roof of his mouth.
◇ The baby's body should face yours so that you're chest to chest.
◇ Supporting the baby on your arm with his body across the front of yours, or under your arm, are common positions. So is lying down with both of you on your side.

How long should feeding the baby take?

You should feed your baby for as long as he likes. Generally a baby can get as much out of the breast as possible within half an hour. After that you can continue while he is sucking effectively, as long as you are both enjoying it – he is probably 'comfort sucking'. Ideally, he should stay on the first breast until he stops sucking and falls off. It is not necessary to time this so he gets both breasts equally each feed.

If you are concerned about when to take him off, or how much he's getting, watch his suck pattern. 'Suck, swallow, suck, swallow' (high flow at the beginning) should gradually change to 'suck ... suck ... suck ... swallow' (low flow at the end). Time to switch breasts or put him to bed.

Towards the end of a feed the milk is richer in fat (and has relatively more calories), so he finds it more satisfying. Indeed it seems that it is the total amount of fat that he gets from the feed that switches off him appetite at the end, not the feeling of a full stomach. Of course if he wants more, then offer the other breast, but if he's not interested, don't worry. Start with the other breast for the next feed, to even things up.

How often should the baby feed?

If we look at other mammalian milks in the animal kingdom (see Part III), we find that there is a relationship between the amount of protein in the milk and the interval between feeds. The rabbit feeds her baby once every 24 hours; the deer has an eight-hourly feed; the dog, four-hourly. Contrary to what you may have been told, human milk is definitely not a four-hourly one. In fact, our milk is relatively dilute, and seems to look like one (brace yourself!) that should be fed almost continually.

If we look at breastfeeding mothers in hunter-gatherer societies, we find that they fed their babies about every fifteen minutes round the clock. Even at night the babies sleep with their mothers and are on and off the breast while the mother sleeps.

This probably represents the 'normal' human pattern. It is certainly the pattern that allows the contraceptive function of breastfeeding to work most efficiently. This is not because the baby is in the way; it's through hormones secreted by the mother's pituitary in response to frequent suckling on her breast!

Our babies grow to be more reasonable in their demands as the days go on, purely as a cultural phenomenon in our society. They do what's expected of them. Some, however, take longer to space their feeds than others. Whether your baby is a frequent snacker or a regular-as-clockwork gorger is just luck.

Remember, however, that the breast fills in about 30 minutes and a full baby's stomach takes about 50 minutes to empty, so he's not being unreasonable if he wants to feed hourly. It usually doesn't take too long before the interval becomes longer.

Let your baby drive the breastfeeding – he knows the way he wants to go. Trying to manipulate his feed times might just make him worse.

The letdown reflex

The ducts that collect the milk produced in the milk sacs of the breast lie deep in the breast. They have muscle fibres in their walls, and under the action of the hormone oxytocin (the same hormone that contracts your uterus), they contract and eject their milk. This explains the afterpains you get in your uterus, especially when you feed the baby, and why feeding the baby soon after delivery is so good to help the uterus contract

In the early days the letdown is often not felt, but it can be detected as a change in the suck/swallow rhythm of the baby as a surge of milk enters her mouth. It also may produce a sudden thirst in the mother – having a glass of water at hand during a feed is a good routine.

After a few weeks, when the breast is less engorged, a mother can often feel this reflex as a tingle at the beginning of (and sometimes during) a feed. Sometimes a hungry cry from her baby is enough on its own to initiate the letdown reflex.

Seven steps to successful breastfeeding

1 Start as early as possible: ideally in the first half to two hours after birth, but certainly within the first twelve hours.
2 Make sure an experienced midwife teaches you how to attach your baby to the breast properly from the beginning.
3 Demand feed the baby right from the start. Give him unlimited access.
4 Feed the baby for as long as he wants to at every feed – within reason. If the feeds are taking longer than 30 minutes a few days after the milk has come in, perhaps he's not attached well or his positioning is wrong so he finds it difficult to swallow.
5 If your nipples get sore, it just means something needs adjusting: either the baby's attachment to the breast or his position. It's not that he's sucking too long or that he's sucking too vigorously.
6 Don't miss the night feeds. It's likely that they boost your milk supply more than daytime feeds. Feeding is also tranquillising, and may help you sleep better.

> Let your baby drive the breastfeeding – he knows the way he wants to go. Trying to manipulate his feed times might just make him worse.

7 Wash your nipples the way you did before the baby. The nipple produces substances that attract your baby and help him attach to the breast, so don't use creams, lotions, potions or that magic ointment that the old lady round the corner says will stop nipple soreness. Change breast pads often and try to spend a little time with your breasts uncovered. Studies show that the best lotion for your nipples, sore or otherwise, is nothing at all.

Issues

It's an unusual mother who experiences no bumps on the road to successful breastfeeding. The important thing is to keep going.

Not enough milk

The more the breast is emptied of milk and the more the breast is suckled, the more milk will be produced. There is a substance in the milk that acts as an inhibitor of milk production, so if there is too much milk left in the breast after a feed, less will be produced next time. Conversely, if the breast is emptied efficiently, it will then go into maximum production. It is a very neat feedback mechanism (no pun intended!). So the best way to increase milk production is frequent, efficient breast emptying. The breast is never completely emptied, though – even following a feed a little milk can always be expressed.

There are few substances you can take to increase your milk flow (called galactogogues). The best is a medication called Domperidone (or the related Metaclopramide), which boosts your prolactin level (prolactin is the hormone that induces milk flow). Other than that, whatever you will be told is myth. No one has ever shown that anything else makes any difference – not stout, brewer's yeast, herbs (with the exception of large amounts of fenugreek) or extra fluids.

Later on, you may notice that your baby has periods when he suddenly starts feeding much more frequently. These are not growth spurts; they are milk induction spurts.

Remember, there are three things that increase your milk supply:

◇ frequent and complete breast emptying (the most important factor)
◇ more suckling at the breast
◇ more rest for mother.

And that's it.

Too much milk

When the milk first comes in, very commonly the breasts become engorged – it could be called the 'beach ball syndrome'. Luckily, this only lasts 12 to 24 hours, and it is largely prevented by rooming in with your baby and giving him unrestricted feeds. If it occurs, it can usually be relieved by cold packs, a couple of paracetamol tablets and gentle expression of a little of the milk to take the tension out of the breast. If the breast is very tight, the baby sometimes cannot attach properly until this is done. Do not attempt to empty the breast; it will just fill up again. And use only hand milk expression machines.

Also, for the whole time you are breastfeeding, use the best supporting bra you can find: one with thick straps and a large enough cup to contain the whole breast. Avoid tight bands across the tops of the breasts – these encourage duct obstruction and mastitis.

Grazed and painful nipples

Many mothers' nipples get 'learning grazes' in the first few days. Luckily the nipples have a very high blood flow, and given a chance, will heal very quickly. So if the attachment to the breast is corrected (sorry to go on about this so much, but you're probably getting the message that it is crucial), they should be pain-free within 24 hours. If you have a cracked or blistered nipple it is a good idea to gently express that breast and feed the baby only on the other side. Then start again on that breast after 24 hours. Only in extreme cases is mechanical expression and feeding the baby breastmilk from a bottle necessary.

Three things increase your milk supply: frequent and complete breast emptying; more suckling at the breast; and more rest for mother. And that's it.

Things not going well

Sometimes, at the start, breastfeeding can seem more trouble and pain than it's worth. The pain from a breast or nipple can be exquisite. This is not surprising, as it is such a sensitive organ even when it's not cracked or chewed and chomped on every couple of hours. Here's a useful piece of advice, though: ***never*** give up breastfeeding at 2 a.m.

In the middle of the night, if things haven't been going well for some days, and you're tired and weepy, and the baby's hungry and howling, and you dread every feed because of the exquisite pain from your breasts, it's easy to just chuck it all in and order the formula. In the morning, though, things often look different, and you may regret your decision … But then you don't want to backtrack … and your mother's happy to share the baby feeding … you're trapped!

Hang in there till morning and make a clear-headed decision in the light of day. Even if it's the same decision, you'll feel better about how you made it.

By the way, you ***can*** backtrack. If you change your mind you can still get your milk back some days after quitting.

Lactose intolerance

Lactose intolerance in a baby who has not suffered a bout of gastroenteritis is most unusual. It is normal for a fully breastfed baby to spill some lactose in his stool. These babies tend to produce rather explosive frothy stools fairly frequently. This usually passes with time, and is not an indication to stop breastfeeding.

If your baby is taking a few very large feeds per day, say four, you could try to feed him more often. This would give his intestine the lactose more gradually, which would improve its absorption.

If your baby tends to 'snack', he might be only taking the foremilk from the breasts. The early milk contains only half the fat of the later hindmilk (but the same amount of lactose), and it's the fat that gives him a feeling of satisfaction and switches off his appetite at the end of a feed. Consequently, though he has a full stomach of milk (and lots of frothy stools, he may not be satisfied. Try to persuade him to feed for longer on the same breast – this way he will get the fat-rich hindmilk and therefore take a smaller total volume of milk.

Burping

Babies are better burpers than we are. The valve between the stomach and the gullet is extremely inefficient in newborn babies, but does develop better tone as the months pass. Many babies have a very poor hold on their feed, and are very likely to posset or regurgitate parts of it during or after the feed. This is even more likely if the baby is postured head down.

So the idea that a baby can trap an air bubble behind this valve, an air bubble that needs ritualised back-pounding to release it, doesn't make a lot of sense. If babies don't burp after they have been fed there are three possibilities:

⬦ the baby didn't swallow any air and there is nothing to burp; or
⬦ he will burp it later by himself; or
⬦ he will absorb the gas.

None of these possibilities is to be feared. Air bubbles in the bowel do not cause pain or discomfort, distension or spasm. Following a feed, all you need to do is to sit the baby up and give him a cuddle – if he wishes to burp, he will. Can you imagine having a satisfying, filling, tranquillising, delightful meal, and then have someone pound you between the shoulder blades before the coffee? It's better to let the baby drift off to sleep and put him gently back in his cot (for more on this see 'Colic and the crying baby').

Vomiting

As mentioned above, the valve between the gullet and the stomach in the newborn baby is extremely weak. If this valve is hanging open as the stomach squeezes to push the milk down into the bowel, the milk is just as likely to be squeezed up and out. This vomiting can even be projectile. X-ray studies of newborn babies show that this is a possibility in most babies, but it improves rapidly.

If it occurs often enough to be a worry or a nuisance:

⬦ sit him up after feeds; or
⬦ put him in his cot in a head-up position. Don't worry, he won't choke. Up to 30 degrees is ideal, but he will tend to slide down the cot unless you put him in a carrying harness with the straps tied to the top of the cot.

What a pity we use the expression 'being sick' for vomiting! Most babies vomit often, and only rarely is it a sign of sickness.

Often, after vomiting, the baby will need topping up right away.

What a pity we use the expression 'being sick' for vomiting! Most babies vomit often, and only rarely is it a sign of sickness.

Twins and more

I know we have two breasts, so we were designed to feed two, but it is a bit of a handful. Under these circumstances you need to be a little bit more pragmatic about the ideology. At night, if one is awake and hungry, wake the other baby and feed them both – either together, if you've mastered the technique of attaching one to each breast, or one straight after the other.

During the day, demand feeding is still worth a try. Often your babies have quite different needs, and trying to fit them into the same pattern won't work very well.

Most mothers can feed both babies entirely on the breast. However, when you're really tired, it's a lot of milk to produce, so keep an eye on the babies' weight gain and get as much help and sleep as possible – any time, anywhere.

Except for the technique of attachment and positioning, your baby needs very little supervision regarding his feeding. Nature is not so dumb as to organise it so that you need three hands, a stopwatch, electronic scales and tubes of nipple cream to successfully feed your baby. The phrase that best describes the ideal process is **baby-led feeding**. Babies will get themselves the right amount of calories if they are offered the breast (often only one is necessary in the early weeks) and allowed to decide when to stop and when to switch breasts.

Our identical twin girls are now one year old. We have learnt that they are double the joy, double the fun, double the laughs, double the cuddles and they are definitely not, to us, 'double the trouble'. Since venturing out in the early weeks with our girls, we realised very quickly that life with multiples was going to be different in so many ways. There weren't going to be any quick trips anywhere any more, not only because of the obvious reasons that there are two, but because there is so much attention paid to multiples by the general community. Everyone wants to see them, touch them and ask questions about them; the fascination can at first be quite overwhelming. It didn't take us long to realise that this is a genuine interest, and is now going to be a part of our life. So for anyone who is expecting multiples, be prepared to take a little longer than expected to shop, pay bills or even go for a walk. Just remember how lucky you are to be part of this special group.

Drugs in breastmilk

Most mothers who are on medication are very concerned that the drug they are taking might be passed to the baby in the breastmilk. Happily, there are very few drugs that get into breastmilk in quantities that have any effect on the baby.

All these ones are harmless:

◇ most common antibiotics
◇ tranquillisers
◇ anti-histamines
◇ analgesics (paracetamol, codeine)
◇ antidepressants (even lithium)
◇ laxatives
◇ antihypertensives
◇ drugs that act on the heart

> The ideal process is 'baby-led feeding'. Babies will get the right amount of calories if they are allowed to decide when to stop feeding and when to switch breasts.

However, **avoid aspirin**.

If you are taking **anticonvulsants**, such as phenobarbitone or phenytoin, you can still breastfeed, but your doctor will make sure that the dosage is correct for you both.

The list would not be complete, however, if we left off **alcohol**, which is fine as long as you don't overdose. Alcohol passes rapidly into milk and rapidly out, clearing in 2-3 hours per drink, so wait 2 hours before feeding. **Nicotine** from cigarette smoke isn't fine at all, and it gets into breastmilk. Smoking has been implicated in increasing the incidence of cot death, childhood leukaemia, respiratory tract infections in the under-fives, and reducing intelligence quotients in smokers' children. So do your little newcomer and yourself a big favour and quit. (If you can't, breastfeed him anyway, as it's still healthier for him than formula and a smoking mum.)

Cannabis dissolves in fat stores (both yours and baby's), hanging about for ages, so it isn't a good idea. *Cocaine*, *amphetamines* and *ecstasy* also can stay in the baby's body for weeks, so steer clear when breastfeeding.

If you are prescribed any drug, you should, of course, tell the doctor you are breastfeeding, just to be on the safe side.

Beware!

These drugs can be secreted in the milk in amounts that affect the baby.

◇ tetracycline
◇ anticancer drugs (antimetabolites or cytotoxics)
◇ long-acting radioisotopes (if you need special X-ray examinations, tell the doctor you're breastfeeding)
◇ antithyroid drugs and iodides
◇ bromide
◇ oral hypoglycaemic agents (for diabetes)
◇ some sex hormones (don't take higher-dose oral contraceptives)
◇ some cortisones (but prednisone is okay in doses up to 80 mg/day)
◇ some antirheumatism drugs (gold salts, indomethacin or phenylbutazone)
◇ antimigraine drugs containing ergot
◇ heroin/cocaine/amphetamines/marijuana.

Bottle-feeding

If you want to bottle-feed your baby, do it. Don't let anybody make you feel guilty about it. Babies prefer their mothers to be well rested and happy. An advantage of bottle-feeding is that Dad and other people can help out; if you are a working mother, this is enormously helpful.

The formulas available today contain a similar amount of nutrition to breastmilk, and babies who are given them will thrive and grow at just the same rate as breastfed babies. The formulas are derived from cow's milk or use vegetable protein from the soya bean. All the different formulas available now – and there are many – contain similar amounts of protein, carbohydrate, fat and minerals as breastmilk. In addition, many also contain extra vitamins and iron in recommended dosages. In choosing a formula, get the one that is easiest for you to get hold of and then stick to it. Don't listen too hard to other mothers' stories or you'll be chopping and changing every time the baby vomits. None of the major formulas make babies vomit (but they all taste awful to adults). Most of them are available in concentrated liquid or powdered form. The liquid form is marginally easier to make up, but rather more expensive.

Mixing the formula

When you use formula, it is very important to keep your hands clean and sterilise the bottle and teat. Set aside a can-opener and knife (for smoothing off the scoops of powder) just for making up the formula, and prepare a whole 24 hours' supply in one go, keeping the made-up formula in the refrigerator. Make up a little more than you calculate the baby actually needs for the day. Boil the water for the formula for a full ten minutes, then let it become lukewarm before pouring it into a sterile jug (or the bottle) and adding the formula powder or liquid. Never add any more formula than is recommended by the directions on the tin – the exact concentration is critical.

Giving the feed

When you feed the baby his bottle, treat the experience as you would a breastfeed. Give him all your attention and, if you like, contact with your skin. He would enjoy it if you took your blouse off and cuddled him during a feed, and you probably would too. You don't need to warm his formula, because babies will take their milk cold just as well, but it's up to you.

How much you feed him is up to him. Just like with breastfeeding, he should be demand-fed, not fed by the clock. If there is something left in the bottle and he's not sucking any more, he's had enough.

On **average** (note the emphasis), a formula-fed baby takes about 170 ml per kilogram (or about 3 fl oz per pound) of his body weight a day, but that's an average baby on an average day. Don't insist on exact amounts each feed. Like us, sometimes he'll want more and sometimes less. Breastfeeders never tell their mum how much they're drinking!

When he's finished, rinse the bottle and teat straight away to remove formula before it dries. Always throw out formula that is left over in the bottle – either at the end of the feed or at the end of 24 hours.

Be careful if you are using a microwave oven to warm formula or to thaw frozen breastmilk. They really heat the milk, but the bottle still feels cold. Always check the temperature of the milk by sprinkling a little from the bottle onto the inner part of your wrist.

I've chosen to bottle-feed my third child, Kaycee. Although this is working well for her, I am finding the feedtime a sharper, less intimate experience than breastfeeding. To compensate, I give us extra contact time – special time spent stroking, cuddling, talking and studying facial expressions. During this time we both love the sharing of eye contact, smell and touch. It is extremely important to me not to miss this beautiful experience. It creates a bond and gives us both comfort and pleasure.

Doing both

If you intend to both breastfeed and bottle-feed your baby – when you are going back to work, or weaning the baby off the breast or, temporarily, trying to build up your milk supply, for instance – you need to be very well organised. Doing both is time-consuming. If a feed takes more than half an hour you will start to run out of time to do everything, so get some help with the bottles while you do the expressing.

Formula does dilute the antibodies in breastmilk that protect the baby from bacterial gastroenteritis, but there are advantages to having even a small amount of breastmilk in a feed: it makes the rest of the formula feed more bioavailable (able to be absorbed), and even tiny amounts of the growth factors and other substances in breastmilk are beneficial. So be organised and do both if it suits.

Travelling

Remember, if you are in a developing country, be very careful of the water supply, and make sure reliable refrigeration is available. Use bottled water if you're unsure of the local supply. Your baby is vulnerable to gastroenteritis if he is bottle-fed. In these circumstances a real effort to breastfeed is worthwhile.

8

How
evolution
designed
our babies

The key to understanding our babies lies back in the mists of prehistory. They have changed little in evolutionary terms since the time we emerged as a separate species.

What has made them the way they are? What kind of society are they expecting to be born into and what are their essential needs? By appreciating our origins and basic biology, we can interpret our babies' language and decode their needs far better than by recycling the tired baggage that babycare has acquired over the millennia.

We're just smart apes

First of all, we are all from the ape family of primates. We have much in common with the other great apes on this planet, but as the story of our evolution unfolds we can see that our differences are as great as our similarities, and the differences are of immense importance in relation to the way we care for our babies.

Let us go back in time, to long before recorded time, to the origins of humankind. You might be surprised to know that the way our babies are today was influenced by the weather in Ethiopia about four million years ago!

The prehuman apes from which our species is descended were tree dwellers at that time, and rarely ventured to the ground. Then the weather became warmer and drier. The top canopy of the trees gradually disappeared, and without the top cover to protect and feed them, the apes had to look for food on the ground. Once they became ground dwellers, they soon became bipeds – as walking upright on their hind legs had a number of advantages.

Two legs, not four

For a start, it was much more energy efficient when travelling, and it gave a better view of the surroundings and thus more warning of attack. It also freed up the arms to manipulate objects – they could make weapons, tools and clothes and carry food from where it was found back to the home base. Being able to carry their food meant that they could now travel further than the local food supply allowed; they moved out of Africa and, as they evolved, colonised the world.

There was one serious downside, though. The whole weight of the body was now supported entirely on the hip joints, and consequently these needed strengthening. Big buttresses of bone developed around the joints to strengthen and support them, but they encroached on the pelvic cavity and reduced the size of the birth canal. The female pelvis became broader than the male's to compensate for this, but there was a limit to how broad it could go: if it was too broad the females' gait would become a waddle, and, in a nomadic society, they may not be able to keep up with the males. In addition, the pelvis was rotated backwards, to distribute the forces of the weight more efficiently, so the birth canal, as well as becoming narrow, also became S-shaped. It didn't matter too much then, as the brains of the early prehuman apes were fairly small – about the size of a hen's egg. Later, however, it began to matter a lot.

Homo sapiens emerges

About 200,000–300,000 years ago there emerged a new and fabulously successful species of great ape which had a big advantage. ***Homo sapiens*** had a big brain and intelligence to match, which would allow him and his descendants to dominate the environment.

But this came at a price. For the first time ever, there was a species that had a high incidence of obstructed labour. The big-brained baby had to be delivered through the same small pelvis, and the more intelligent he became the harder it was to push him through the fixed and inflexible ring of bone. Nature found itself with a big dilemma. How to fix it?

The solution was obvious, and we're still paying for it. The only way to get these babies out before their heads were too big to fit through the narrow birth canal was to have them earlier in the pregnancy, when they were actually still premature. In this process, nature stripped off as many of the instinctive functions as possible before thrusting the babies out into their parents' arms.

Our premature babies

This is essentially our problem: we have the most premature babies of all the great apes. Chimpanzees have 45 percent of their brain formed by delivery – we poor humans have a mere 25 percent.

And how did Mother Nature intend to make up for this immaturity and lack of instinctive ability? You've guessed it. She dumped the problem on you, the parents.

Long childhood

In addition, our babies, more than any other mammal babies, require intense, prolonged and complex parental care and supervision for years. I hate to break this to you, but if you think you're going to get away with less than 20 or 30 years of total dependency, think again! And even then they won't move out unless you move into a one-room apartment!

As you can imagine, the effects of this heavy childcare responsibility on the species have been immense. The emerging human society had to contend with babies that needed protection, nurturing and training over many, many years. Aspects of the culture, and even the biology, were subjugated to the need to provide a stable family within which the helpless infants could be reared successfully.

The development of human society

In most ape communities, strong alpha males control most of the females in the troupe and have little to do with the offspring; they spend most of their time maintaining their power base and keeping young pretenders at bay. The females do all the baby care – the male only offers physical protection (and only if he is reasonably sure the babies are his).

With the greater needs of its immature babies, and their long childhoods, the emerging human society found itself being driven towards a different kind of community from that of other apes. Evolution started heading towards the pair-bond, towards a system of human couples forming a nurturing and secure environment for their children, and it did so by using sex.

Using sex to select a society

Male apes tend to have little interest in the females unless they are sexually receptive, which is around their time of fertility. Evolution therefore started selecting for females to have a longer period of sexual receptivity, and even extended this time beyond when they were fertile. Sex started to become used to enhance the bond between pairs, not just to produce babies. So successful was this at forming secure and lasting relationships between males and females that gradually the human female became sexually receptive full-time; with this, the monarchical alpha male system collapsed – now every male could have a mate.

As the male became surer that any babies his mate bore were his, he invested time in them, and hunted specifically for his family.

Sex for meat

He needed to! One effect of continuous sexual receptivity was that human females developed frequent menstrual periods, and they were heavier than those of any other mammals. Other animals lick themselves and retain the

valuable iron in the blood. Being bipeds, it was impossible for humans to do this, so the possibility of iron deficiency emerged.

A deal was struck between the human females and males: sex for meat. The hunter male had to bring home iron-rich meat to maintain the health of his mate and their infants.

> Sex began to be used to enhance the bond between pairs, not just to produce babies

The hunter-gatherer community

In the new human society of the Pleistocene era, there were small groups of nomadic 'hunter-gatherers'. These groups were made up of about nine to fourteen people. There would be two or three fertile women, a couple of older women, some children, a baby or two, and the men. The group would wander about, collecting food as it went. Tasks were divided up and food sharing became the norm.

Males developed the attributes of hunters – the ability to plan a hunt, the daring to carry it out, and the skill to throw missiles accurately – so that they could obtain the protein and iron-rich food that was so badly needed by the women.

Women: the backbone of the society

The women gathered most of the staple food for the group. The most was collected by the postmenopausal women, and the least by the teenagers (little has changed!). Women developed the ability to find food, share childcare, and nurture each other and the community; they developed new attributes, such as altruism and generosity. They became multi-tasking, networking carers.

In addition to the prolonged nurturing that the human infant required, female humans also needed special care. In the period after their difficult labours (and this is also unique to humans among all the mammals), the females found it hard to take care of themselves, and required help from others for food and protection.

Help from alloparents

Now that there was no longer a fertile period, the babies came along at any time of the year, not all at the same time as in other species. This gave the group the opportunity to focus their efforts on only one or two babies at a time, and gave the mother support. There were unencumbered females (called 'alloparents' by anthropologists) who could give mothers respite from continual care of the baby. Just as well, too, as the babies had to be carried all day and needed frequent feeds to meet their growth needs.

So daycare was a reality even then. Significantly, though, it was 'daycare by kin', by people who had a personal investment in the baby and his family. Such 'division of labour' and co-operation developed community spirit which helped form a society with enough long-term stability to support the slowly developing babies.

Babies' needs: then as now

So the helpless, premature, vulnerable human baby is born one cold night into a hunter-gatherer community. What are his needs, and what systems has evolution devised to make sure he gets them fulfilled?

His needs are clear and unchanging:

◇ food
◇ warmth
◇ protection
◇ sensory input.

Let us look at each in turn and examine how each is met.

Food and feeding

For the human baby, breastfeeding has always been of paramount importance for survival. Like all mammalian milks, human breastmilk is unique in its structure, and has the perfect combination of food, growth factors and anti-infective properties to exactly meet his specific needs. It is designed to grow a very large brain in as short a time as possible, to give the baby lots of water, and to offer protection against infection from the outside world.

Primate breastfeeding: human style

Anthropologists have observed the feeding habits of babies of the hunter-gatherer groups that still exist, and the results are very revealing.

The mothers breastfeed their babies very frequently. The baby snacks for about two to three minutes, sometimes as often as every 30 minutes, whenever mother is available. During the day the females gather food and the baby is passed around the group, so the frequent feeding is often interrupted, but at night, the baby has the mother's undivided attention. Once the group has found shelter and settled down, the babies sleep close to their mother, skin to skin, now feeding almost continuously. This is the time when babies can concentrate on feeding, as mother is undistracted and no one else is involved with his care. So the feeds become even more frequent at night than during the day. I am sorry to report that humans are, by nature, night feeders! This is confirmed by research that shows that night feeds lead to higher levels of the hormone that induces milk flow (prolactin) than day feeds do. As a consequence, a mother can maintain her milk flow by just feeding at night; this is less easily done by just feeding during the day.

So when your young baby calls for a night feed, that's what he needs – and he's helping maintain your milk flow! Sorry!

The contraceptive effect

Apart from the excellent nutrition this provides, this pattern of frequent feeding has a very important contraceptive effect. The hormone prolactin is also very effective for preventing ovulation – as long as the breasts are stimulated often, around the clock. If the baby sleeps for longer periods, it rapidly becomes inefficient, and absolutely cannot be relied upon! In the hunter-gatherer communities, it successfully spaced children out to about one every four years, as babies were breastfed for two to three years. Studies of these communities also revealed that this seemed to be the most efficient spacing as far as longevity and family size went. It seems that in those circumstances the female who produced about six children during her reproductive life ended up providing more surviving children than those who produced more or fewer babies.

Human breastmilk

What is so special about human milk, and why do babies feed so frequently? We get a clue when we study the concentration of the constituents of human milk and compare them with the other mammalian milks in the animal kingdom.

The main nutritional components of milks are fat (a high-calorie energy food), lactose (a special carbohydrate), protein (for building cells), and solutes (phosphorus, calcium and sodium, i.e. salts). Each component seems to have a special function, and the combination tells you much about the specific needs of the baby.

⬦ **Fat**: Babies who need high-fat milk are usually big animals born into cold climates. The blue whale, for instance, has milk of 50 percent fat; the seal's is not much less. Both of their offspring grow at a tremendous rate and need to maintain a thick layer of fat. With such thick, treacly milk the baby whale can hardly suck at all – the milk is just injected into its mouth, like an aircraft refuelling in midair. The deer has about 22 percent fat, the dog about 8 percent. Man (originating in the warmer or temperate parts of the globe) is much the same as the cow or goat, at about 4 percent.

⬦ **Lactose**: Lactose is brain food. It is the dense and energy-rich carbohydrate that is essential for the growth of nervous tissue. It forms galactolipids (such as cerebroside) that are present in large quantities in the brain and form the substance of the brain. The bigger an animal's brain (in relation to body weight) and the more brain it has to grow (this will depend on whether the animal is born very immature), the more lactose there will be in its milk. Cows and sheep (not bright animals) have 4 percent. Humans are top of the heap with 7 percent: they have big brains and immature babies that still have a lot of nervous tissue to lay down. Interestingly, seals have none, not because their brain is small (they are really quite bright animals), but because their brains are almost fully formed before they're born.

⬦ **Protein**: The protein quantity in milk tells us many things about the animal. The higher the protein level in the milk, the shorter the gestation, the quicker the rate of growth and the shorter the animal's life. Also, the higher the level, the less frequently the young animal feeds. For instance, the rabbit has up to 13 percent protein in the milk: it has a short gestation (28 days), doubles its birth weight in six days, and lives about five years. It feeds just once a day. Reindeer have 10 percent protein in their milk and feed their young every eight hours; dogs have 7 percent protein and feed their puppies every four hours. Human milk has a protein content of only 1–2 percent. It is clear that humans belong to the animal group called the 'continuous-contact species': that is, their babies feed almost continuously.

⬦ **Solute (salt) load**: Another interesting aspect of human milk is its very low 'solute load' – that is, the small amount of calcium, phosphate and sodium (salt) in it. The amount of salts in the milk usually parallels the amount of protein; the left-over chemicals of all these substances have to be excreted through the baby's (immature) kidneys. This process removes water wastefully from the body. Having a low solute load/low protein milk also helps a baby survive in a hot, dry country. Much of the water can be used for sweating and keeping the body cool by evaporation instead of wasted excreting leftover chemicals through the kidneys. It is easy for such babies to remain hydrated when they hang around their mother, feeding much of the time.

⬦ **Fluid**: We need to give our babies about 170 millilitres per kilogram body weight a day if they are to get enough food to grow optimally. They actually only need a 100–120 millilitres per kilogram body weight a day to stay hydrated under normal conditions.

So when we breastfeed we are giving our babies almost twice as much fluid as they need. No wonder they wee all the time! And no wonder we do not need to give our breastfed babies any extra water, even in the hottest weather, as long as we give them unlimited access to the breast. Studies done in the Sinai Desert (ambient temperature 43°C) showed that babies continued to pass lots of dilute urine as long as they were fed on demand.

Four-hourly feeds?

It looks as if human milk was never designed to be fed to our babies every four hours. That rumour got started because if the baby isn't around his mother all the time, smelling and sensing her, he will demand feeds less often. The baby's stomach can accommodate about a sixth of his necessary daily supply at one time. So, if you give six feeds a day (that is one every four hours) he'll get enough food, but remember, this is a cultural choice, not a biological requirement.

Brain food

Only 25 percent of a baby's brains are formed at birth. The rest of the thinking brain tissue needs to be laid down in the next eighteen months – and the clock is ticking. If this window is missed, for instance in famine or because of severe illness, the potential for full brain development is lost forever.

Because its brain is growing so rapidly, the human baby needs almost continuous nutrition. Human breastmilk was designed precisely for this, as it is high in carbohydrate and low in fat and protein. The fats are interesting, too. Breastmilk contains special long-chain fatty acids that are not present in other milks; these are taken up by brain cells to make important constituents of brain matter.

Other components

The milk also contains other substances, the purpose of which we do not yet understand: growth factors, hormones, and enzymes abound. Most of their functions are obscure, but nature wastes little, so we can assume they *have* a function even if we have not yet discovered the how, where or why of it. Breastmilk's 'bioavailability' is also very high – that is, every component is absorbed and used by the body. It is a truly amazing food!

Breastmilk and future IQ

In full-term babies it is hard to prove the superiority of breastmilk over formula in relation to later intelligence. Recently, however, exhaustive studies have shown a small but significant advantage for the breastfed. This difference in IQ also seems to increase further if breastfeeding is prolonged.

However, if one studies the premature infants in our intensive care units, then the evidence becomes clear. There was a study of premature babies in a UK intensive care unit about thirty years ago. Half the babies were given banked breastmilk (which is calorie poor because it has been stored) and the other half were given normal formula (not the formulas especially developed for premature babies that we have now). The difference in later IQ, psychomotor, and social development was obvious, and became more obvious the smaller and more premature the baby was. For instance, the average IQ difference at 32 weeks' gestation was about 8 points. Even more interesting was the results from the smallest (24 weeks' gestation), growth restricted, male babies. Their scores were up to 30 points down! That is not a subtle difference. Breastmilk is serious brain food.

You can also see why 'premature formulas' were developed – to make up for the difference between formula and breastmilk in an era when breastmilk banking lost favour because of the worry about cross-infection.

> Only a quarter of baby's brain is formed at birth; the rest is laid down in the first 18 months

Warmth

Unlike other apes, our babies are born naked, without fur. They would soon die from hypothermia without the transferred warmth of the mother's body in a skin to skin embrace. From very early times babies were dressed in animal skins to keep them warm.

Human babies are also born with special pads of brown fat between their shoulder blades. This fat's sole function is to be broken down and provide warmth should the baby become cold. These stores last long enough for feeding to become established and the baby's basic metabolism to begin providing warmth. But transferred maternal warmth remains an essential source of energy for months after birth.

Baby fat

Interestingly, the human baby is unique among great apes in the amount of fat on his body at birth. Even the vast silverback gorilla produces a scrawny infant with no more than 2 percent fat on his body – the human baby is often a bouncing 15 percent! Delivering our babies is difficult, and adding a thick layer of fat only makes it harder, so the fat is likely to have an important function. Just what it is, though, we don't yet know. It may be useful for warmth and insulation (though early man dressed his baby in skins and fur). It may also act as a store of energy to boost brain growth (though babies often get even fatter after birth), or perhaps it is merely a relic of our aquatic past. Most attractive, though, is the suggestion that it is part of the baby's many mechanisms for encouraging his parents to love him – he is making himself as cuddly and adorable as possible. It is certainly true that the bigger the baby, the more confident and relaxed the mother feels about her infant. This reason has my vote.

Touch

One of the basic requirements for primate babies is the cuddle. We are a 'continuous-contact' species. Not only humans, but other apes, require skin to skin contact in order to develop properly. I guess it's not surprising. For millions of years, being separated from one's carer for more than a short time meant death. Primate babies still live with this primordial terror of being abandoned. They need the constant reassurance of a familiar, responsive carer to give them security and confidence. The need is overarching and unsubtle. Their basic neurological system is designed to respond to, and evoke, close contact and attachment. Babies automatically curl their bodies and cram as much skin as possible against a warm embracing body. Their lips root for and encircle a nearby nipple and their senses drink in the sounds, sights, smells, tastes of the mother's body. For the first weeks and months, this is the baby's environment. Not the family, home or country – just mother's body.

Skin-to-skin contact

Studies with premature babies have shown that skin-to-skin contact with a carer improves the physiological state of the babies, regularising their respiration and soothing them. In the developing world, premature babies in hospitals do better if they are regularly given 'kangaroo care', that is, skin-to-skin contact with the mother. Full-term babies, still relatively premature, are no different. They need cuddles like fish need water. Such contact reassures them and seems to be necessary for normal neurological and psychological development, and for them to become securely attached to their parents and carers.

Nature also knows that if babies were to be abandoned, it is likely to happen in the first few days. After breastfeeding is established, the bond between the mother and baby rapidly becomes too firm to break. Indeed, breastfeeding has many hallmarks of an addiction: the body of the mother and the baby secretes morphine-like hormones as a response, inducing them both to come back for more. But even before this bond is fully formed, the baby has started to work his magic, making sure his mother will envelop him in affection and love. To induce all that selfless devotion (and sheer hard work), the newborn needed to focus many aspects of his development on attracting and interacting with his mother and father. In effect, he became a sophisticated love-inducing machine.

> The baby's environment is not family, home or country, just Mum's body

Monkey babies and touch

Experiments with monkeys confirm this need for body contact. Monkey babies become miserable, distressed and listless when they are separated from their mothers, even when they are fed well. One research study a few years ago separated infant rhesus monkeys from their mothers. It offered the baby monkeys a choice: in their cages there was a warm, mother-sized terry towelling-covered tube with a face painted on the top, or a similar-sized tube made of bare wire through which poked a bottle teat that delivered milk.

The monkeys preferred to cuddle the terry towelling tube, and sucked on the teat as briefly as possible, and only when they were very hungry. They preferred the security of a warm cuddle to food. This was emphasised by a later experiment. In this, the mother-substitute did unpleasant things to the clinging babies (blowing cold blasts of air at them or poking them with a spike), and still they clung on, even more tightly.

Other studies have shown that monkeys separated for a few days from their mothers at the equivalent age of a toddler also were distressed on separation. However, when they were reunited, the baby monkeys regressed in their behaviour and became very clingy with their mothers, hardly trusting them to be out of their sight for a moment. If mum looked as if she might leave they would throw a tantrum and become angry and agitated. Months later they still weren't themselves. They were anxious, wouldn't explore like the other monkeys, seemed depressed, and were timid about changes in their cages.

How securely attached the baby monkey was to his mother before he was separated seemed to be a very important factor for these monkeys.

The secure ones fared better than the ones who harboured suspicions about the possibility of their mother leaving them.

Insecure attachment

Long-term studies of infants who in toddlerhood were shown to be 'insecurely attached' (that is, very anxious about brief periods of maternal absence) showed that this played an important part in the ease with which they fitted into the school environment and later formed personal relationships. It seems that the seeds of personal confidence and self-esteem are sown in the nursery.

Protection and care

Our immature baby is born in a very vulnerable state, in need of a great deal of protection and care. His hands are made only of cartilage and his arms have no strength; unlike other apes, the human baby can't even hold on to his mother's body – he must be carried. He can barely even support the weight of his heavy brain on his scrawny neck at birth. No wonder the carry sling was invented 200,000 years ago, especially by nomadic people! This had a profound effect on babycare, as it allowed a mother to continue to work while remaining constantly in contact with her baby, offering the protection and warmth of her body.

Within the tribe there were only a few babies at any one time, so there were always women who were unencumbered (alloparents) – older females, single girls and other fertile females – who could help mothers with the day-to-day tasks of childcare. In nature, the usual situation is that once an animal's reproductive capacity disappears, it dies. This is not so with the female human. Women live for decades beyond the menopause, because they are an essential resource for the family and they are needed to help with babycare.

However, none of these alloparents was invited to breastfeed. Nowhere in the animal kingdom is breastfeeding routinely shared. Breastmilk has high concentrations of antibodies to germs. These antibodies are created by the mother's body to ward off specific germs in her particular environment. So her milk is a custom-made cocktail for the protection of her own baby, who is there with her in the same environment.

How babies subjugate parents

Nature was not so foolish as to deliver these premature infants into the hands of their parents without making sure that there was a good reception waiting for them. Evolution put in place numerous little mechanisms to make sure that the parents rapidly attached to the baby and worked for her survival.

Within minutes of birth the baby lets her parents know that she knows them and their instincts automatically respond to her primordial prods. By setting up the baby's senses to respond to her parents, nature ensured that they quickly responded to her too, and recognised her as their responsibility. So her nervous system was programmed to respond to and subjugate her parents to her survival needs.

After I had my third baby I became very defensive about him. I didn't want any visitors, not even my other children. I just wanted to go to the back of a cave and give him all my attention, without distraction.

Vision

Observe any baby in the first few hours after delivery. Many parents are astounded that the baby scans the room, finds their faces and gazes at them fixedly. This is not an illusion.

Facial attraction

Testing shows that she actually has an instinctive preference for the human face over inanimate patterns. She even prefers good-looking, symmetrical faces to the unattractive. And your instincts interact with hers. When she locks her gaze onto yours, you are programmed to come in close to her focal distance (about 17 to 20 cm) and to talk and respond to her. This is all part of her little plan to make sure somebody falls in love with her (hopefully her parents), takes her home and loves her forever. It usually works, too.

Pattern preference

Following this period the baby loses her intense interest in looking around and becomes more interested in the touch of her mother's skin, her breasts, and her milk. When she is about four weeks old, the intense gazing returns. This is why people once believed that a baby could not see for six weeks. This is not true. Though it is hard to get her attention, it is possible, in these first weeks, to get her to interact with you.

Choose a time when she is quiet and alert. When presented with a definite facial expression she will attempt to imitate it. Give her a big smile or stick out your tongue. Often you can see her tentatively try to do the same as she gazes at the expressions on your face. If you move a bright object around at her eye level she will follow it within a 30° angle from side to side. She has a definite preference for patterns with rounded curves and soft lines rather than sharp zigzags, and she likes light and dark contrast in patterns. She also has some power of colour discrimination –

she can separate red from green, but it will be some months before she can pick out blue from other colours.

Hearing and auditory memory

Recent research regarding the sounds that babies relate to and remember is fascinating. Firstly, babies hear well. But have you noticed that when you speak to a baby you instinctively speak in a high voice to get her attention?

Indeed, babies do prefer higher frequencies and discriminate between them better. This may be due to the fact that a mother's voice is higher-pitched than a father's and, in the womb, the baby hears it more clearly.

Sound recognition

Babies also respond to their mother's voice, as distinct from another woman's voice, from the earliest moments of postnatal life – it makes their heart beat faster. Specific response to the father's voice takes a few days.

It also seems that sounds to which the baby has been exposed in the last month of pregnancy produce a positive response after birth. In one study it was noted that unsettled babies quietened when the theme tune from 'Neighbours' was played in their presence, if their mothers were regular viewers of this TV program, but not otherwise (the other babies probably screamed louder!). Even more interesting was a study that had mothers reading a rhythmic children's poem (Dr Seuss's *The Cat in the Hat*) to their babies in the womb. After birth, the babies sucked harder on a teat when that particular poem was read to them but not when another poem with an identical rhythm was read. There was clearly more to it than just a response to the rhythm of the sounds; other auditory cues seemed to be important.

Harking back to the womb

In essence, new babies respond to sounds they heard in the womb. The loudest sound in the womb, however, is not voices – it is the pounding of mother's arterial system. Most mothers carry their babies on the left side, whether or not they are left-handed. They know that the baby is calmed by the sound of their heart, a deeply familiar sound, harking back to the womb. So when we want to bounce or pat the baby, we instinctively do so at around the maternal heart rate. Babies quieten more effectively to beat of about 70 a minute than to a faster or slower rate.

Many years ago, when I was pregnant with my boy, I went to see the movie *The Guns of Navarone*. During the big battle, the baby in my womb was going crazy with the explosions – I nearly had to leave the cinema. Twenty years later he joined the Army and became a demolitions expert!

Smell and taste

Smell plays an enormous role in reproductive matters in much of the animal kingdom. The females of many species secrete substances called pheromones – these attract a mate or indicate that they are ovulating. Some secrete pheromones onto their nipples to guide the young to feed. Smell also seems to make sure some animals don't mate with members of their own family – the 'family smell' repels them. A fair amount of research has been done to see whether such agents are important in the human mother and baby, helping them bond or enhancing breastfeeding.

Baby smelling mother ...

There is no doubt that the foetus inside the womb can smell and taste. Of course, in the watery environment of the amniotic fluid these two senses are one. Within the amniotic sac the baby spends much of her waking hours swallowing large volumes of the fluid. This is absorbed into her circulation and hence to her mother's, via the umbilical cord, and is also urinated out at a high rate.

> Anything that reminds babies of their time in the womb will calm them

Tasting amniotic fluid

Foetuses can be encouraged to swallow even larger volumes of fluid if it is sweetened with saccharine and less fluid if is flavoured with an unpleasant taste. So we seem to be born with our 'sweet tooth' already developed.

Conditioning to tastes and smells before birth

Foetuses can be 'conditioned' to tastes, too. An interesting study showed that if mothers were given the spice cumin to eat for a week before they gave birth, after delivery the newborn would be attracted to that smell. This implies that the foetus can develop smell/taste recognition before birth. That shouldn't be so surprising. Many animals learn what tastes 'good', that is, what is healthy to eat, by tasting it in the amniotic fluid before birth. Remember, babies (animal or human) in the womb are gulping the fluid most of the time, and in the latter part of pregnancy they have all the equipment to discriminate tastes and smells (which are similar, related senses). After birth these animals will reject anything they meet that has an unfamiliar taste. They therefore avoid eating harmful foods even if their mother isn't around to tell them. The study mentioned above shows that human babies may have such discrimination, too.

In case we didn't already know, anything that reminds babies of their time in the womb tends to calm them, at least at first. Babies will quieten in the first few days when presented with the smell of their amniotic fluid. They even suck more avidly on a nipple if their amniotic fluid has been applied to the nipple. This preference for amniotic fluid disappears at about four to six days, when the preference for the smell of mother's breast emerges.

And after birth

Experiments have shown that breastfeeding babies recognise and have a preference for the smell of their own mother's breast-pad by six to seven days of age, and a day or so earlier they show a preference for that over a clean pad.

If a mother wears a certain perfume during breastfeeds, within a day that baby will turn to the smell of that perfume and expect a feed. Midwives have known for years that it is not a good idea to change your perfume once breastfeeding is established, as it can confuse your baby.

Though babies can taste, they are not too discriminating about taste preference. They will certainly reject tastes that most humans find unpleasant but they cannot be relied upon to protect themselves from harmful substances – for example, in a tragedy many years ago, formula that had accidentally been heavily salted was still taken avidly by the babies to whom it was offered.

The varying taste of breastmilk

Babies' tasting ability brings up another important advantage of breastfeeding. Within the womb the foetus gulps vast quantities of amniotic fluid each day, actively partaking in mother's diet and getting to know her taste preferences. After delivery, she would prefer that situation to continue. How sad for the baby whose mother takes advice from the dear old lady over the road who suggests that, 'Now you're breastfeeding, dear, you have to be very careful about what you eat. I suggest a diet of rice and peas.' Suddenly the baby's enjoyment of taste experiences contracts as her diet goes bland. She wonders where the chilli, the garlic, the rhubarb, has gone. Where also is the forbidden pleasure of chocolate?

There may be something innate about the baby's preference for various taste experiences. A small study indicated that garlic eaten by mothers and secreted in the breastmilk (where it could easily be detected by smell) encouraged increased sucking in their babies, and that the babies consumed more milk per feed. Alcohol made the babies suck more avidly, but they took less milk. So one of the beauties of breastfeeding is the variety of taste sensations that your baby enjoys, unlike her formula-fed companion, who gets the same boring taste, month in, month out.

The taste experience that lasts a lifetime

It is not too surprising that breastfed babies, once weaned, enjoy the taste of new foods much more than formula-fed babies do – and eat twice as much as formula-fed babies! Another study of a random group of five-year-olds who were given a vegetable they'd never seen before showed that the kids who had been breastfed were found to be more likely to try it than the formula-fed kids.

But the effects can last even longer. A group of university students were given a questionnaire, which asked if they enjoyed eating or thought it was a bother; and if they enjoyed it, whether they preferred familiar dishes or new ones. The answers divided neatly into the breastfed ones (liked eating, tried new dishes) and the formula-fed (found eating a chore and were reluctant to taste new dishes).

The effects of our babyhood ring down through the years in many ways.

... and mother smelling baby

Ask a mother about the smell of her baby and a dreamy expression will waft over her face; she will use the words such as 'intoxicating, delicious, wonderful ...'

A fascinating study in Israel described how at a maternity hospital, straight after birth, the newborns were all dressed in singlets. After 24 hours the singlets were removed and placed in sealed bags. After three days each mother was presented with three sealed bags and was asked which singlet belonged to her baby. As long as a mother had had more than 12 hours' contact with her baby in the first 24 hours and she was a non-smoker, she recognised her baby's smell 100 percent correctly. Such recognition seems, in the early days, to be even more accurate than recognition of the sound of the baby's cry or her face in a photograph.

Our archaic sense of smell

The sense of smell is our most primitive, and the nerves from our nose go directly to the oldest part of the mammalian brain, with very few intermediary connections. We all know that smells can evoke multi-dimensional memories, memories that arise complete and unbidden in a way that memories aroused by other senses don't. So it is not surprising that smell profoundly influences such basic functions as reproduction. We also know that as far as smelling ability goes, girls beat boys hands down at any age, from birth to senility. In mature females, it also seems to vary with the menstrual cycle, and pregnancy also tunes it up considerably. Some women know as soon as they're pregnant, because suddenly they can't bear strong smells such as bacon or coffee.

Family smell

Rats will avoid mating with those who are close family when they recognise a 'family smell'. Fascinatingly, their smell and their immunity are very closely linked at a molecular level. The gene locus (the place on the chromosome) for immunity is just next to that locating the smell characteristic. Recent research has also shown the same phenomenon in humans!

Women were given a bag of dirty T-shirts worn by men and asked to line them up in the order of smell attraction (or rejection!). When the results were correlated, the order showed that the women preferred the smell of the T-shirts belonging to strangers over those belonging to family members. On analysis of the immunological characteristics of the men and women it was found that the women preferred the smell of those men whose immunity was most dissimilar to their own, and rejected those who were closest (family). One can deduce that we wish to have babies with as strong an immune system as possible – this would give the babies a greater chance of fighting infections – and we know that this is achieved by getting different characteristics from both parents.

But there's more. These women were given a tray of 36 basic perfumes that have been used in the industry for millennia: musk, citrus, rose and so on. They were asked to name their preferences. Women of similar immunological characteristics chose similar perfumes. Perhaps we choose perfumes that we know innately will enhance our family, personal smell. The take-home sentence: you can't buy perfume for your friends – but you probably can for your family!

Choosing a mate

By the way, it seems that this family odour is altered by sex hormones. So if you're choosing a mate (I guess this book is a bit late for you here), you might want to stop taking the pill before making your final decision …

Nipple pheromones

The nipple of the rabbit secretes a powerful scent that attracts the rabbit pup and encourages her to attach to the nipple and to suck. This substance is a chemical that can be diluted to one part in 20,000 and still be a powerful attractant. It is also volatile, which means that it evaporates over a few hours and the effect disappears. These substances are called pheromones – these are hormones that are secreted onto the surface but do their work at a distance from the body.

> Smell and immunity are closely linked at the genetic level

The case for a human nipple scent

The question of whether the human also secretes a breast scent that attracts the baby to the nipple has been researched in depth, and the answer is a resounding 'probably a little'! It is logical that animals such as the rabbit or pig have such a system: their young are sightless and the mother can't physically help them to the breast, so they need good inherent guidance to reach their food supply. Humans don't have that problem. In addition, many of the animals that have a powerful scenting system for breast attraction are those that are all born at the one time, such as lambs. As there may be hundreds of lambs in the same paddock, they need a good recognition system to get to their own mother's nipple.

Humans in small groups in which there are only one or two babies (as in the hunter-gatherer group) do not have this issue to deal with, so have little breast scent.

Detailed tests to see whether the human baby has a similar innate attraction to the lactating breast came up against a couple of problems. First, as mentioned, boys' sense of smell is not very sensitive, so the studies were done with just female babies. Second, babies will recognise a specific smell within 24 hours if it is accompanied by a feed, and will turn to the smell in expectation of a feed. So to detect a smell as subtle as a nipple pheromone, only girl babies who had only been formula-fed were used. After all this, the research shows that there is a preference to the lactating over the non-lactating breast. The bottom line is that the nipple does secrete some attractant, but it is subtle. However, it is logical not to wash your nipples before feeding, or to bathe them only in water, not soap (as the attractant is probably a fat).

Sleeping with your baby: myths and truths

P eople who sleep with their babies in their bed nowadays generally keep very quiet about it. If they don't, everybody gets on their case. They are told by friends and strangers that they'll never get any sleep, that their babies will develop sleeping problems and that the child won't survive as it will be 'overlaid' and smothered. None of these statements is true. And many parents do it anyway, love it, and keep it a family secret. The following is the truth about it.

The evolution of closeness

After the hunter-gatherer, what then? How did we get to where we are today, with our questions and uncertainties, our fierce debates about the politics of daycare and mothering? Where did the feeling come from, that somehow, some time ago, the relationship with our baby got thrown out with the bathwater of history.

For millennia following the Pleistocene Age, babies continued to stay close to their mother during the day and sleep with her at night. Then, in Europe in the fourteenth century, problems started to emerge with this model. Social conditions started to change. The family and tribal units started to disintegrate. Marriageable men became scarce, and the ones who were available had little money. This was a time when there was no social safety net, no protection for the poor or the unwed.

'Overlaying'

Between the fourteenth century and the eighteenth century there was a pandemic of neonatal deaths. Thousands upon thousands of newborns died of 'overlaying' – they were smothered in bed with their mothers, apparently accidentally. It was so common that, retrospectively, we can see that it became one of the major factors in population control for that part of the world (the others being war, famine, disease and celibacy).

But the Catholic Church and governments were not fooled. The babies who were lost were, at least before the seventeenth century, usually from poor families who had more children than they could cope with, or from single girls. This was a time when life was short and brutal. Marriage occurred late because jobs were scarce and money was in short supply for most of the population – and marriage, in this sexually repressed era when unwed mothers were not tolerated, was essential for the support of babies. There was no social security or support network to help if unwanted babies arrived. The Catholic Church knew what was happening, as, during confession, the truth would emerge. The priesthood knew that this was not accidental 'overlaying'. This was infanticide. So, in an effort to stop the carnage, the Church banned parents co-bedding with their babies.

Governments also tried. The Italians banned co-bedding unless a little cage (called an 'arcutio') was used which covered and protected the baby in the bed. Not surprisingly, this didn't change the death rate at all.

Foundling hospitals

In the end institutional pragmatism surfaced with some governments opening 'foundling hospitals' – starting with the Italians in the fifteenth century. These were hostels where desperate mothers could leave their babies, if their circumstances made it impossible for them to care for their babies. These hostels were well used. By the mid-nineteenth century, 43 percent of babies born in Florence were abandoned to such institutions. Other European governments opened similar institutions through this period in an attempt to stem the epidemic of infanticide. Sadly, from the seventeenth century onwards, many middle-class and wealthy couples also decided to opt out of parenting and availed themselves of this service.

The hostels were, by any standards, a total disaster. They became overcrowded, and the death rate of the babies reached levels of 95 percent in some places; the babies mostly died from gastroenteritis, as there were not enough wet nurses to feed them and no safe artificial feeding alternative.

Why am I telling you this sad and sickening tale? Because it gives us insight into the reasons behind a strong cultural belief. It is a 'given' in our society that it is unsafe to sleep in the same bed as a baby. We have a deep belief that our bodies can be lethal weapons to our babies. It still remains in our consciousness that 'overlaying' is a potential problem.

> By the mid-nineteenth century, 43 percent of babies born in Florence were abandoned

The Industrial Revolution

In addition, the Industrial Revolution arrived in the eighteenth century. Suddenly babies were not wanted in the family bed, as both mother and father had to get up early in the morning to go to work in factories and mines. Babies became second-class citizens, and the baby's finely designed mechanisms for giving itself a warm secure environment until mature enough to leave mother's side were ignored. The baby was placed in a cot, and moved into a separate room.

Closeness today

Let's leap forward in time and see where we are with this today.

The fortress nursery

Following World War II the prevailing view in Europe was that new mothers could not be trusted to manage their babies without the help of professionals. The 'fortress nursery' was in its heyday. You could visit your baby for 20 minutes every four hours to feed him, but then you had to leave. When you left the hospital they handed you your little stranger, and you went home and did the best you could.

Rooming in

However, in the early 1960s the Swedes experimented with the radical view that perhaps mothers might be able to manage safely with the babies cared for in the mother's room. It was immediately successful. 'Rooming in' had arrived.

Later came low-tech deliveries, early breastfeeding, the 'bonding' concept and an appreciation that mothers mostly need to be given confidence and encouragement – they need only a little in the way of information to manage their babies competently.

The final barrier

The final barrier to caring for the baby as he was designed to be cared for was very resistant to assault. Paediatricians and other experts strongly advised (and many still do) against having a baby in an adult's bed, and suggested that it was the cause of a number of problems, from death by 'overlaying' and Sudden Infant Death Syndrome (SIDS) to childhood sleep disturbance and psychological problems in later life.

Bed-sharing research

Research done in the early 1990s by a team led by Professor James McKenna – who is, significantly, an anthropologist, not a paediatrician – has opened up the whole question about the advisability of sleeping with your baby and this work is worth examining in some detail. He was aware of a body of research that indicated that newborn babies may not be well equipped to sleep on their own. It had been noted that babies appeared to benefit from 'arousals' that is, periodic gentle stimulation to prevent them dropping into the deeper realms of sleep. Such arousals would be common when a baby was close to another person in bed.

The studies

He and his team undertook detailed studies of mother and baby pairs: he studied mothers sleeping with their babies for one night, and on another night he studied them sleeping in separate rooms. All night, all their physiological functions, such as heart rate and respiratory rate, and sleep characteristics, such as eyeball movement (an indicator of sleep) and EEG (brainwaves), were monitored and recorded. They were also filmed with night infrared video, to watch their activity.

The results

The studies and his conclusions make fascinating reading. The babies behaved differently when in bed with mother than when the two slept apart. When the two slept together the babies appeared physiologically more stable, with fewer obstructive pauses in their respirations during the deeper levels of sleep. Their sleep patterns were especially different. Neither the babies nor the mothers spent much time in the deep levels of sleep (so-called level 3), but hovered in twilight and dream sleep for most of the night (levels 1 and 2). However, both mother and baby slept for longer periods of time overall. They also synchronised their sleep patterns – when one awoke, so did the other, both initiating 'arousals'. There was constant activity and interaction between baby and mother. Baby would sidle up to mum, take a quick feed then settle, and later mum would pat him, adjust his clothing or cuddle him. They spent over three-quarters of the night face to face and there was a constant interplay of actions and reactions between the two. The babies were contented, fed more frequently and never cried.

'Sounds good', I hear you say. 'But how did mother feel about the lighter sleep and the constant activity?' Answering a questionnaire, mothers overwhelmingly reported that their night's sleep was as good or better with their babies than when they slept in separate rooms.

Conversely, when these same mothers slept in a separate room from their babies, the babies fed less often. When they did, though, the babies' demands jerked them both into full awareness, as mothers went next door to feed and settle the baby. Also, when the mothers were alone in their beds, they had a higher level of anxiety regarding the health and wellbeing of their baby. Though both did drop into deep sleep, on average their sleep patterns were more disrupted, and, by the mothers' report, less satisfying.

The conclusions

The conclusions bore out what we would expect, given babies' evolutionary past and their premature state: the babies seemed to benefit from the presence of their mother close to them during sleep.

These findings regarding sleep patterns suggest that co-bedding babies ought to have a lower incidence of cot death (SIDS), as the presence of level 3 sleep and lack of arousals (see above) have been implicated in SIDS. It was therefore a surprise when epidemiological studies from Tasmania and New Zealand showed a marginally increased incidence of SIDS in co-bedding pairs! Re-analysis of the data showed that when the influence of alcohol, drugs and smoking were eliminated, the incidence of SIDS was not increased.

The relationship between bed-sharing and **reduced** SIDS incidence has never been proven in any study, but it remains a tantalising possibility.

Do you want to bed-share?

Many mothers wish to sleep with their babies, but most of them keep quiet about it, as our society's norm is to emphasise the dangers and warn against it. So, before you embark upon it, it is important to examine your reasons for wanting to do it. The commonest reason to want to do it is because it just feels right and is very enjoyable, yielding a contented baby and mother. It also enhances and promotes breastfeeding. Many mothers who co-bed successfully like the fact that they sleep in a twilight zone, aware of their baby even as they sleep. Throughout the night they remain confident of their infant's health and wellbeing, and they totally discount the possibility of overlaying their baby. But it's not for everyone, so if you don't feel it's for you, don't give it a second thought.

Actually, most families that do bed-share probably never plan it at all: it's just the way things pan out with that particular baby.

We really enjoy co-bedding with our new baby. I'm a little worried that the baby will get too used to it, but my husband especially enjoys it and wants to continue. The baby sleeps between the two of us on top of the blankets, and we both sleep much more lightly than we used to.

Check out your sleeping arrangements

It's very important that parents examine their sleeping arrangements to make sure that if bed-sharing happens, it happens safely. Beds in the twenty-first century home are not the same as in the Neolithic, and many adult arrangements are not suitable for an infant. Parents should also be aware that no sleeping arrangement is totally safe, and that nothing so far known will completely eliminate the possibility of SIDS. Since the early 1990s, the incidence has definitely been reduced enormously by sleeping baby on his back. No other single factor has had as great an impact on SIDS rates as this, but a residual level remains, at about 0.87 per 1000 births, and this seems hard to reduce further. Parents embarking on bed-sharing must understand this issue clearly.

◇ The bed must be firm and large (a King-size is ideal).The bed should be firmly against the wall or a firm bolster should lie between the edge of the bed and the baby so he cannot slide off the mattress and asphyxiate between it and the sheets. Mattresses on the floor and couches and sofas are especially dangerous.

◇ There should be no soft pillows, and no heavy bed coverings that may smother the infant. Duvets/doonas are dangerous.

◇ Toddlers are not safe in the bed with infants and will have to move to their own bed.

◇ Most important, when they sleep, the parents should have their wits about them. That means no alcohol or drugs that would cloud the protective response to their infant. For the same reason they shouldn't bed-share when they are dog-tired, as this will also put them into the deeper non-protecting realms of sleep.

◇ Another absolute prohibition in co-bedding is cigarette smoking. If either parent smokes the baby should sleep elsewhere. For some hours after the last cigarette potentially lethal gases are exhaled and these can a real danger to the baby. Environmental smoke is bad for babies in many other ways other than increasing the likelihood of SIDS. So if you haven't given up by now, this is a good time!

The above are the most important rules, but there are a few others as well:

◇ No waterbeds – they interfere with the baby's ability to control his temperature.

◇ If the baby has a temperature or is sick, he should stay in his own bed.

◇ No soft toys or bumpers in the bed. There should be nothing that can cover your baby's face and interfere with his breathing. Also, if either of the parents has long hair, it should be tied up.

◇ No obesity. If either of the parents is significantly overweight this can reduce their sensitivity to locating their infant safely within the bed.

A cot next to the bed

Remember, many organisations say that the safest place for a baby is in a cot next to the family bed. I don't dispute this. With that arrangement there are fewer rules, and more margin for error. There is also a device you can buy that clips onto the side of the parental bed like a cot-sized bed extension, allowing the baby to have his own area.

If you want to bed-share, do so, but stick to the rules

Parents who wish to co-bed should do so, but they must stick to the rules. It is just another way for parents to enjoy their baby and for their baby to enjoy them. Many parents will start the night off with the baby in his own cot then, at the 3 a.m. feed, bring him into the big bed for the rest of the night. Most babies also nap in their cot during the day – it is unusual to have babies who are not familiar with and comfortable in their cot.

When to stop

When to stop bed-sharing is another hornet's nest. Suffice it to say that at five months the baby can develop manipulative behaviour patterns. 'If I cry now I can get Mum here. I don't need anything but, hey, let's give it a go!' By this time breastfeeding is well established, so it might be time to try a little persuasion to get the baby to stay in his cot.

Having said that, I have been inundated with mothers with five-month-old infants asking me 'Do I have to stop? We're both having such fun.' This is purely a matter of family choice. If you all enjoy it, keep doing it – it can only improve your relationship with your baby. However, do check with your partner to make sure he's not feeling left out. He may need more cuddles, too.

And for those looking for an exit, there is usually another window of opportunity at about a year, when infants seem to look for more independence. Try it then.

The bottom line is, don't be browbeaten into putting your baby in a cot to sleep if you want to feel his warm soft body against you in your bed as you doze quietly. Stick to the rules, but go for it!

Bed-share if you want to, but stick to the rules

> I was depressed after the birth of my first three babies and needed antidepressant medication. This time I took my baby into my bed and we slept together for the first few months. I found the experience positively euphoric. My little boy didn't cry in all this time and we just had the best time. I didn't come down from my high for months. I cried when he wanted to go into his own bed!

Bed-sharing rules

- ◇ no alcohol
- ◇ no drugs or sedatives
- ◇ no cigarettes
- ◇ no extreme tiredness, exhaustion in parents
- ◇ no water-beds or mattresses on the floor
- ◇ not if your baby is ill or has a temperature
- ◇ beware the edge of the bed, and avoid falls and entrapping between mattress and sheet – make sure the bed is against a wall or there is a firm bolster between the edge of the bed and the baby
- ◇ no duvets or doonas; in winter, warm the whole room
- ◇ no bumpers, soft toys or bed-clothes that can cover the baby's head
- ◇ no sleeping on couches or sofas
- ◇ no toddlers in the bed as well – put them in their own bed
- ◇ no animals
- ◇ no long hair – tie it up
- ◇ no great obesity.

11

Settling in at home

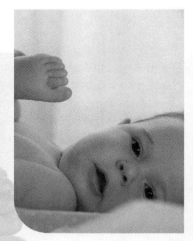

Most first-time mothers can't wait to get home after having their babies. Most second-time mothers have to be prised out of their hospital bed and sent home, kicking and screaming! There is a lesson here for first-timers. Remember, not only does the housework await you, but when your friends visit, they now expect to have a cup of tea and wake the baby for a cuddle. They usually stay too long, too.

There are a few things to think about before going home. Your anxiety level about your baby is likely to increase. Also, you will probably rush around a lot more, so you will be more tired, so your breastmilk supply will diminish slightly over the first day or two. The combination of these factors is likely to make your baby behave differently for a few days, and this can make both your anxiety and your fatigue worse.

My advice therefore is to expect a change in your baby's behaviour and accept it. Remember that his behaviour changed from day to day in the hospital and will continue to do so at home until a pattern is established.

Also, ignore the housework, or get someone else to do it, and rest as much as possible.

Siblings

Imagine how it must be. You are two years old and the supreme ruler of your family. One day your parents bring home a baby, a young pretender to your throne, and Mummy, your personal slave, starts giving this intruder a lot of attention. And to add insult to injury, he regularly sucks on her breasts, which up to now have been your private property.

Your plan of action:
◇ Become a baby again – demand a dummy and require a daytime nappy.
◇ Do everything in your power to divert Mummy, especially during feeds.
◇ Be as naughty as possible – after all, *any* attention is better than none.

Bringing home a new baby means major lifestyle change for a previously only child, and this has to be sympathetically appreciated and planned for.

In the hospital, make sure all the things you need to do with the baby are done before the older sibling arrives. This will allow you to give all your time and attention to the older child. If the baby cries or plays up, try to ignore it or leave it to dad.

> Siblings under 20 months do not seem to mind a newcomer as much as those over 20 months. The nearer the child is to three, the easier it will be. But two-year-olds are trouble.

When the time comes for you to leave the hospital, big sister or brother should come to help you take the baby home, but should hold your hand while Dad carries the baby. The worst thing you can do is send the older child away to a grandparent when you bring the baby home. You will be sending the child a clear message about whom you now prefer.

Use your common sense, and make looking after the baby a joint project. Give the older child a baby doll of his or her own to look after, and get the child to help with the baby – even if each task takes twice as long. Try to get the older child to help with the decision-making: if the baby is crying, make a joint decision about what to do about it (big sister can't stand the noise either). Shower the older child with affection. Try to make him or her feel a real sense of responsibility for their little baby. If both are crying at the same time, try to comfort the older sibling first.

Siblings under 20 months do not seem to mind a newcomer as much as those over 20 months. The nearer the child is to three, the easier it will be. But two-year-olds are trouble.

Friends

For the first few days after you go home, your real friends will stay away – if they do show up, they bring dinner and take your toddler to the park! As for the others, do not wake the baby for them. Be polite but firm and give them some housework to do. With any luck they will remember an urgent appointment.

Sleep

Next to feeding, sleeping is the subject that most concerns new parents (their own as well as their baby's!).

A baby's sleep requirements vary enormously. Studies show that the range lies between eight and 22 hours per 24 (with a 'typical' baby sleeping about sixteen hours per 24) in the first week after birth. This period shortens only by an hour or so during the rest of the first year, but the pattern changes.

Young babies sleep almost as much during the day as the night, but as they get nearer to six months the night-time sleep gets longer and the daytime naps become fewer.

Don't worry if your baby seems to sleep for only short periods of time. The babies who sleep for 23 hours a day and wake up only for feeds are usually other people's babies. Some babies spend most of the daylight hours watching their mother, blinking at the light and generally enjoying all the activity around them. Some babies don't like to nap – but when they are awake, they whinge. Some babies sleep during the day and howl all night. It takes all kinds!

> Don't worry if your baby seems to sleep for only short periods of time. The babies who sleep for 23 hours a day and wake up for feeds are other people's babies.

A common piece of advice given by helpful bystanders is: 'Keep him up during the day and he'll sleep longer at night.' WRONG! Actually, it's the reverse. The longer a baby sleeps during the day, the longer he'll sleep at night. This is because if he sleeps for more of the day, there's less opportunity to stimulate him, so he'll be less stressed and he'll sleep even longer. Reduce the playtime to increase the sleep time.

Generally speaking, tired babies sleep. If that's not enough for you, try the manoeuvres in the chapter on 'Colic and the crying baby'. Remember, no baby has ever become sick from lack of sleep – only his poor parents have.

Mother, not martyr

It takes some effort to juggle everyone's needs and take care of yourself at the same time when you arrive home with a newborn baby. Don't forget to do these, though:

1 Eat normally and regularly. If you are breastfeeding, your weight might diminish as you transfer your fat deposits to the baby (and might not if you eat enough for two). It is important, though, to have a good nourishing diet to provide for you both.

2 If you are obsessive about housework, try to get some help with it. This is no time to clean, wash and scrub. If you can't get help, let the house go a bit and instead enjoy the little spare time you have.

3 As fathers have not gone through delivery, they may not fully understand that it takes some weeks for you to recover your strength, quite apart from the nocturnal demands made on you by a little baby. Sex may be the last thing on your mind in these first weeks, but it may be uppermost in your partner's. The most vital sexual activity for you both at this time is to talk about it – don't just avoid the subject. Then when your libido starts to return you won't find a cranky, jealous mate who feels he's been jilted in favour of a baby.

Babies have a few critical needs: the most important is a happy mother and father in a stable and loving relationship. This part of baby care needs as much attention as the nappies.

In fact, don't be surprised if recovery takes longer than you expect. A follow-up study of over 400 mothers found that sexual problems such as decreased libido, discomfort with intercourse and difficulty reaching orgasm reached their peak at three months after the delivery, with four out of ten women affected. Half of these women continued to have these problems for over a year.

The study also showed that, though many of the physical problems were resolved in the first month, breast problems, haemorrhoids, dizziness, fatigue, hair loss and constipation sometimes persisted for three to nine months after delivery. Mothers in the first year after having a baby also have an increased risk of catching respiratory infections such as colds and flu.

From partner to father

It cannot be coincidence that so many diverse cultures exclude fathers from the birth process. It is as if they fear that the father might get too involved in his newborn baby and neglect his role as provider. It just would not do for Dad to spend all day playing with his baby by the hearth when there is no food in the kitchen. Studies of fathers' responses to their newborns seem to validate this conclusion. Most fathers who were very involved in the birth process exhibited much the same behaviour as mothers when presented with their babies – some took quite a dominant role in handling and playing with the baby. Certainly, they seemed totally engrossed with the little one and positively bursting with self-esteem. You can usually recognise a new dad: he's the one with terminal fatigue in his smiling muscles.

It must be said that a father cannot be as involved with his baby as a breastfeeding mother. Babies tend to treat their fathers with indifference for a few weeks, as they are mostly interested in the smell, taste and milk of their mother. Most fathers can handle this without getting upset or jealous, but it is a good idea to involve the father as much as possible in all the caretaking activities he **can** do. Literally, the more he does for the baby, the closer he will feel to him. This is one of the few advantages of bottle-feeding: it allows the parenting role to be divided more equally between mother and father.

Babies have a few critical needs: the most important is a happy mother and father in a stable and loving relationship. This part of baby care needs as much attention as the nappies.

Superdad

Some early studies on parent attachment assessed the closeness of the relationship between mother and baby through describing the way the mother behaved while the doctor examined her baby. If she stood on the other side of the room gazing out of the window, and when the baby cried, turned around and muttered, 'Oh, he's always doing that', she scored a big zero. If she stood next to the doctor and immediately pacified him when he cried (the baby, that is – doctors are pretty brave), she scored a six.

I recently had a big burly dock worker and his wife in my consulting rooms for their baby's checkup. The mother had been quite sick, and had had to remain in hospital for four weeks following the birth of her baby. Hence the husband had looked after all the baby's needs and had bottle-fed him. When I examined the baby, I had to contend with an enormous shoulder in my way – father got a score of seven out of six for attachment!

Fathers get attached, too

As a young neonatologist in the US, I once flew 480 km (300 miles) with the Newborn Transport Team from Denver to a small town in Kansas. We were to pick up a baby girl who had become sick a few days after birth.

When I arrived, I met the parents and reassured them that we would stabilise the baby and then fly her back to Denver Children's Hospital. It took about an hour to stabilise the little girl, then we took off. As we wheeled the baby in through the doors of the Denver Children's Hospital, the father was there to greet us. He had beaten our flight to Denver in his car – and had received only one speeding ticket! He watched over her cot until she was out of danger.

I learned something when my first baby was seven weeks old that wasn't in any book or suggested by any midwife. It's nothing that helped my baby sleep or eat or cry any less, but it made a difference to me. A baby's 'grasp' reflex keeps their hands and toes bunched up for months, and an amazing amount of sweaty, smelly, salivary fluff builds up in their palms. Use some cream while they're in the bath to slip your fingers through theirs to clean them out. The result is a clean and sweet-smelling fist to suck on!

Out and about

You can go stir-crazy if you're stuck in the house with a baby for days on end. Soon you just have to get out. The motion of the pram can also put the most unsettled baby to sleep. Take him to the park!

Driving

It is incredible how many unrestrained children one sees in the back seats or, worse, the front seats of cars. These presumably loving parents are obviously unaware that with the slightest deceleration of the car their child becomes a missile so heavy that the strongest man could not hold on to him. Anyone who has ever worked in a children's intensive care unit will tell you of the agony of parents who are completely unharmed after a minor collision and whose child has gone through the windscreen and now lies broken or dying in hospital.

Children need to be restrained in cars for every journey, no matter how short the journey is.

> Children need to be restrained in cars for *every* journey.

It is now the law that your baby must travel in a restraint device in a car. The best one for small babies is a rear-facing safety capsule. Get if fitted as soon as, or before, you go into labour – it needs to be there when you take your baby home from hospital. Quite apart from the safety aspect of the first drive home, it gets you into the habit of never having children or babies in the car unless they are fully restrained.

If your child strongly resents being strapped in, it is a good opportunity to teach him some discipline – he needs to realise that some rules do not change and are not open to negotiation.

Like child abuse, there is never any excuse.

Leaving babies in the car

You've all seen the newspaper reports, but it's worth repeating here. In warm weather the temperature in a car can rise to lethal levels in just a few minutes. Even 'popping into the shop' is dangerous and unsafe. Spending an extra three minutes to get the babies in and out of the car is nothing when bottomless and endless misery may result if you don't.

Flying

Aeroplanes are pressurised to an atmospheric pressure equal to that at 1600 metres (5000 feet), so it is perfectly safe to take even your newborn baby to see his relatives overseas. If he was born prematurely and had severe lung disease you may need to wait till he's back to full health before flying.

It is, in fact, a good deal easier to travel with a newborn baby than it is with a toddler. Babies do not have the constant need to move around and can usually be comforted with the breast or a feed. They also do not kick the chair in front, spill every drink handed to them, need to go to the toilet only when the food trolleys are blocking all the aisles or become fascinated with the hair of the man in the seat in front.

Pressure problems in the middle ear when the plane is descending are probably less common in babies than they are in adults, as the Eustachian (connecting) tube between the pharynx and the middle ear is much shorter in babies. Nevertheless, when the plane descends, it is worthwhile getting the baby to suck, as this will equalise pressures around the eardrum. Pilots do not always tell you when they start their descent, though – it is often an hour before arrival. Ask the cabin staff to let you know. Strictly speaking, it does not really matter if the baby becomes upset because of the pressure in his ears – he will yell if he's upset, and that is the best treatment to equalise the pressure. His noise should not worry your fellow passengers, as their ears will also be affected by the descent!

There was a rumour a little while ago that long haul flying was associated with an increased likelihood of cot death in the days following. Detailed studies were conducted and it was shown not to be the case, but some babies were found to be sensitive to the slightly decreased amount of oxygen in pressurised aircraft and this altered their breathing pattern. The sensitivity disappeared once they were back on the ground. Keep a close eye on your baby when in a plane, but you don't need to worry about SIDS any more than usual.

Later medical matters

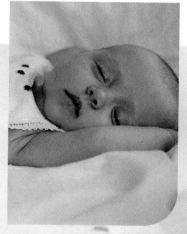

Once you leave the hospital, you're on your own. You wish you'd asked more questions. Even little things seem to assume catastrophic proportions deep in the night. The little rash becomes a major indicator of disease, the crying a call of acute distress …

Remember: all you need to look after a baby successfully is common sense and trial and error. And one or two facts. Here are some useful ones …

How much weight should the baby put on?

◇ Most babies in their first months will put on 180–200 g a week once feeding is established.

⋄ A lower weight range (160–180 g a week) should only be accepted as satisfactory if the baby is contented. If the baby is not happy, check the feeding, perhaps with a lactation specialist or midwife, just to make sure things are okay.

⋄ Most babies who are gaining less than 160 g a week, no matter what their behaviour is, would prefer a little more feed. Talk to a lactation consultant or a breastfeeding association counsellor to get things onto a more solid footing.

Nappy rash

The sensitive skin of a newborn baby can suffer a number of problems, mostly minor ones. Remember, dermatologists' and paediatricians' babies get nappy rashes, too. It does not reflect upon the quality of your care of the baby.

Nappy rashes can be divided into three general types:

Contact rash

This rash occurs in areas that are in contact with the nappy (the creases of the thighs are unaffected). It is mainly caused by irritation of the skin, from moisture in the nappy and also by substances in the urine, like urea, forming ammonia after being broken down by germs from the baby's stool.

Treatment

1 Wash the nappies in commercial preparations of gentle, non-enzyme detergents and rinse them carefully, or try disposables for a week or so (studies have shown that disposable nappies cause fewer rashes than cloth nappies, so they aren't a bad option anyway).
2 Stop using soap on the baby: use a non-soap cleanser with pine tar oil instead. Use pure petroleum jelly or a cream containing zinc and castor oil at first.
3 If there is no improvement, see your doctor. He or she may prescribe half or one percent hydrocortisone cream to use at each nappy change.

Once the rash has improved, use a silicone-based barrier cream to protect the skin.

Rash in moist areas

This rash tends to be worse in the creases of the skin, though it may be uniform throughout the nappy area.

Treatment

Use the same management approach as for the contact rash, but remember, this rash may be caused by thrush or have thrush superimposed on it.

1   Use an antifungal cream such as miconazole or clotrimazole.
2   If it doesn't improve in a day or so, see your doctor, who may prescribe some hydrocortisone cream with an antifungal agent.
3   If either this rash or the contact rash refuses to go away, stop using lanolin (in moist towelettes or baby lotions, for instance) altogether.

Excoriated buttocks

This rash occurs around the anus and looks just like a burn, which is exactly what it is. It is caused by the liquid stools from (usually) breastfed babies in their early days. The stool of these babies is very acid (lactic acid from the leftover lactose), and, especially if the stool is frothy or fluid, can burn the buttocks.

Treatment:

1   Change the baby's nappy frequently.
2   Give the area a thick layer of petroleum jelly or silicone-based barrier cream before you put her nappy on.
3   Leave her exposed to the air when you can.

Eczema

'Eczema' means 'scaling'. This rash occurs in a mild form on the cheeks of many babies, usually from four to ten weeks of age. It's called 'seborrheic eczema', and it's due to overactive sweat glands adapting to life outside the womb. The skin of the cheeks becomes rough, red and spotty; the rash can spread behind the ears and on to the chest. Many babies also develop scaliness of the skin under the hair and eyebrows. This is called 'cradle cap'.

There is also a more severe form that usually runs in families that are atopic (that is, families that have an allergic tendency). The baby can have more intense scaling and cracking of the skin, and over a larger area. In addition, weeping and redness caused by infection to the skin of most of the upper body can occur, especially behind the ears, on the back of the neck, the face and the chest. And this rash can be very itchy. Babies will usually grow out of this in the first six months or so.

Occasionally, this kind of rash tends to last for longer – even blending into adult-type eczema as the child grows.

Treatment

The treatment is directed to diminishing the activity of the sweat glands.

1   Stop using soap when you bath the baby. Use a non-soap cleanser containing pine tar oil. If the rash is severe, limit bathing to a couple of times a week.
2   Stop using fancy baby lotions and creams. Moisturise the skin with sorbolene, with or without glycerin, and use half or one percent hydrocortisone cream from your doctor in all but the mildest cases. This steroid cream is perfectly safe for babies and can be used liberally. It is the mainstay of the treatment, but is only used to get rid of – or if severe, minimise – the rash.
3   Once you get ahead, stop using the steroid and go back to a moisturiser.
4   Try not to use brushed synthetic fibres or wool next to the baby's skin.

If the rash is more than mild, have it treated by your doctor.

Cradle cap

Cradle cap is (seborrboeic) eczema of the scalp (or eyebrows).

1   The mildest cases will resolve with sorbolene.
2   It responds well to petroleum jelly, which softens scales and allows their removal.
3   It is also worthwhile trying a tiny amount of antidandruff shampoo now and again, as this is also likely to help.

If it is more severe, take your baby to the doctor. The doctor will probably use steroid cream and limit bathing.

Waxy ears

After a few weeks, babies sometimes start to produce liquid wax from the ears that stains the pillow. This is usually from ear canals that get wet in the bath and aren't dried enough. The ear then produces more wax, to protect itself. The trouble is, a warm, damp ear canal is a great place for skin bacteria to multiply, so the ear can also get infected and smelly.

After a bath, if the inside of the ears have become wet, dry them gently with a twist of soft cotton wool inserted into the canal. Do not poke anything stiff – such as a cotton bud – into the ear.

Sun kicks

Sunlight should really come with a warning: 'In overdose, this radiation is harmful to your health. In sufficient dosage, it may even be lethal.'

> When your baby goes out in summer, she should always have sunscreen on exposed skin and wear a hat or bonnet with a brim.

Sun kicks are quite helpful for people who:

◇ live in the northern hemisphere, where the radiation is lower;
◇ have a diet short of vitamin D; and
◇ have heavily pigmented skin.

It is rarely relevant in Australia – babies here should be exposed to the naked rays of the sun as little as possible. To see small babies sunbathing naked on beaches is a sad sight – quite apart from the long-term possibility of skin cancer, babies can burn badly in minutes.

When your baby goes out in summer, she should always have sunscreen on exposed skin (the sunblock lotions for babies are completely safe) and wear a hat or bonnet with a brim.

The days of worshipping the sun are numbered. It will surely soon be fashionable to have porcelain skin (and no wrinkles until you're 60!).

Oral thrush

Babies have immature immune systems, and many of them are not able to withstand infection with a common environmental fungus called *Candida albicans*, better known as thrush. This usually occurs in the mouth, and looks like white milk curds stuck to the inside of the cheeks. Unlike milk, though, it cannot be scraped off. It can also occur on the baby's gums and palate; however, a white-coated tongue is usually not thrush. Thrush can cause soreness but most babies are pretty tolerant of it, and only rarely does it cause a feeding problem.

Treatment

1　The fungus can be removed by nystatin or other antifungal medicines (such as miconazole gel) put in the baby's mouth after she has had a feed.
2　It is also worthwhile putting some antifungal cream on your nipple after breastfeeding to stop cross-infection.
3　If you are bottle-feeding, be very careful with sterilisation of the bottle and equipment.

The thrush is never resistant to these antifungal agents, but it is sometimes difficult to eradicate because of constant reinfection from the feeding equipment. So change the sterilisation fluid you use for dummies, bottles and teats even more often than usual until the infection starts to come under control.

Reflux

'My baby vomits all the time and brings back everything I put into her.'
'Is she putting on weight normally?'
'Yes, but ...'

The mother of a baby who has (gastro-oesophageal) reflux can be recognised by her harassed expression, the nappy permanently on her shoulder and the smell of sour milk that accompanies her wherever she goes.

Frequent vomiting is a nuisance, and can be demoralising. All that beautifully produced milk dumped on the shoulder of your dress or saved for Daddy's trousers when he gets home! The vomiting may be effortless or projectile, and the baby will often be hungry afterwards.

All newborn babies reflux to some degree. There is a valve between the gullet and the stomach that works very poorly in newborns, so the milk may go up and down the gullet like a yo-yo after a feed. In some babies, it comes out of the mouth, in other babies it does not. Reflux can become problematic when:

◇　the amount of vomiting becomes more than a nuisance
◇　the baby does not put on enough weight
◇　people start blaming the baby's crying on the vomiting, saying the baby has 'heartburn' (see 'Colic and the crying baby').

Don't panic – the majority of babies will grow out of their reflux problems, usually in the first four months. The question is, can you wait that long?

Also there is a body of evidence that suggests that the symptoms of reflux are vomiting and vomiting. Not pain and not irritability. These are usually caused by other issues (see 'Colic and the crying baby') that may well increase the amount of vomiting and cloud the issue. Also 'silent reflux', causing irritability without vomiting, is an unusual phenomenon under three months of age.

Treatment

1   The first thing to do is adjust the baby's resting position. The best posture – to empty the stomach and keep the feed as far away from the gullet as possible – is with the baby on her right side and head up at about 30 degrees from the horizontal. For bad cases, it may be worth propping up the head of the cot on blocks and placing the baby in the cot in a carrying sling that is secured at the head of the cot.
2   Some doctors recommend using an antacid to reduce the irritation at the lower end of the gullet after each feed; some also prescribe a medication that stops the stomach producing acid (ranitidine).
3   If the reflux is bad in a bottle-fed baby, it is definitely worthwhile thickening up the feeds with carobel or a proprietary milk-thickener. The formula companies now produce 'AR' (anti-reflux) formulas that have thickener added. Later on, the introduction of solids can do the same thing.
4   Drugs such as cisapride are not generally prescribed now, as their side effects are significant and they haven't been shown to work on closing the valve between the gullet and the stomach effectively.
5   Only rarely is an operation to make the valve more efficient necessary.

Bowel actions

It's hard for a childless person to believe, but parents can wax positively poetic about the quality and quantity of their beautiful baby's poos. The strange thing is that their comparisons are always culinary, such as 'peanut buttery', 'pesto-like' or 'seedy'.

Breastfed baby

For a breastfed baby, once meconium has been passed and the milk is in, anything from 20 stools a day to one every two weeks is normal. The stool can be yellow, green or brown, or any combination of these. It can be fluid, seedy or pasty. For breastfed babies, it is never hard. I have never met a normal breastfed baby who was constipated, that is, passing hard stools (constipation is not infrequent stools).

If you are worried that your baby has not passed a stool for several days, when she eventually does pass it, check its consistency. If it is anything other than rabbit pellets, it is normal.

Breastfed babies who produce stools at long intervals can seem uncomfortable on the day, or perhaps the day before, they produce them. You will soon get to know your baby's patterns and accept this as okay. Breastfed babies never need any help to go more frequently. So put away the petroleum jelly-covered cotton bud, the suppositories, the stomach massages, and the prune juice. Think of the money you're saving on nappies!

If your baby is producing loose, frequent, opaque yellow stools, she is spilling a little lactose in her stool. Babies can spill as much as 10 g per litre of lactose in their stool. This is normal – it does not indicate lactose intolerance.

The only stool that should cause you concern is stool that is as watery as urine. Under these circumstances it is wise to seek medical advice, as the baby may have gastroenteritis. Breastfed babies are immune to bacterial gastroenteritis, but can still get a viral form of the disease.

Bottle-fed baby

Bottle-fed babies tend to have rather firmer stools and to pass them between four times a day and once every two days. The colour tends more to the rustic browns and greens than to the Van Gogh yellow.

It is certainly possible for bottle-fed babies to become constipated; this is indicated by hard stools rather than infrequency of stools. If the stool is firm or hard, add a little maltogen or brown sugar (one to two teaspoons) to the baby's bottle or offer her a small amount of prune juice – this will normally be enough to soften it. Sometimes well-diluted orange juice and extra water will be helpful. Don't use suppositories for your baby without your doctor's approval – it is almost never necessary.

Diarrhoea

Loose, watery stools in any baby should be treated with respect – they might indicate gastroenteritis. Even fully breastfed babies can get this, especially from a virus called rotovirus.

Unlike the normal loose stool of many breastfed babies, the stool that indicates diarrhoea is 'urine-like' and resembles water. If you're unsure, check with your doctor. The main danger from diarrhoea is dehydration, which can occur rapidly, because babies' bodies have only small reserves of fluid. If your baby is still wetting three nappies a day there is no immediate danger.

Go and see your doctor anyway, as this problem does need medical attention. Take a sample of the stool with you. To collect one, line a nappy with a plastic bag so the fluid is also caught. If you have to wait very long for the stool, it's probably all right anyway!

Breastfed babies can usually continue feeding normally; bottle-fed might benefit from a change to a lactose-free formula.

Lopsided head

Now that we place our babies on their back to sleep, the incidence of SIDS has dropped enormously. There is a small downside to this sleeping position, though. Quite frequently babies' heads develop an asymmetrical shape, with a flattening of one side of the back and a slight bulge at the front. Its medical name is 'plagiocephaly'. It causes no harm to the brain at all, but as the weeks turn into months it can become fairly obvious. Why does this occur?

Babies' heads grow at a phenomenal rate – about a 1 cm in every fortnight in the first few weeks.

Right from the start, babies develop a strong preference to look to one side, especially when they are asleep. Perhaps it was the direction they were looking in the womb, perhaps it's because their mother normally carries her baby on her left side where her heartbeat can be heard. Most babies also have a preference to look towards the light, which might mean your baby faces the window in her room.

Whatever the reason, the baby may face one direction much more than the other. The baby's skull bone is quite thin (about 1–2 mm thick), and it contains a heavy brain. When you combine these things, it's easy to see why the head grows asymmetrically: the back of the head on the weighted side becomes flat and the forehead opposite starts to bulge outwards.

By six weeks it can be obvious, especially if you look from the top of the baby's head down. When it is pointed out to them, parents can be quite surprised by how misshapen the head has become in such a short time.

The good news is that with good management the head can re-shape in about the same time. You just need to change the baby's posture so that her head looks the other way:

◇ Move the cot so that the window is in the direction you want the baby to look.

◇ Put a small roll of a cloth nappy under the shoulder on the same side as the flattening. This will throw the baby's head over to the opposite side.

◇ Posture the baby more onto her side, but be careful: up to a fifth of babies placed on their sides (in one clinical study) ended up on their front (a big no-no because of cot death). Her side posture should only be slight, so that if she struggles, she rolls onto her back, not onto her front.

It's worth working at this. The head grows very fast in the early months, and will remodel the flattened head quickly. Also, in the first months you have some control over her sleeping position. After five months, you have none – she'll sleep however she likes!

There are two other reasons for a lopsided head, so it's probably a good idea to take the baby for a checkup with your doctor anyway:

1   Your baby may have a sternomastoid tumour. Before you panic, the word 'tumour' is Latin for 'lump', and in this context it has no connection with cancer. A sternomastoid tumour is a swelling in the strap muscle that connects the sternum (breast bone) to the mastoid process on the skull (just behind the ear). This muscle can be stretched and bruised during delivery, and this can cause the lump and the shortening of the muscle. It can also cause the baby to prefer to look to the opposite side to the shortened muscle. This condition usually needs physiotherapy to stretch the muscle, but it gets better in a few weeks.
2   Your doctor might want to take a skull X-ray of your baby's lopsided head – there are rare cases when such asymmetry occurs because the sutures (or joints) at the back of the skull fuse too soon.

Remember, though, that no matter how wonky your baby's head looks, it does no harm to the brain within.

Questions and answers

Being a first-time mother is by definition a new experience, full of tasks to be learned and problems to be solved. In light of this, there is no such thing as a stupid question. Use these questions as a basis for your own list, writing down any others as they occur to you.

Q. If she vomits some of her feed, should I top her up again?
A. That depends on her. If she appears willing to suck, top her up; if she does not seem to be in any hurry, wait for her to demand a feed before putting her back on the breast.

Q. Should I clean my baby's ears? Is there a safe way to do it?
A. It is not a good idea to immerse your baby's ears in water, as the canal is difficult to dry and can get infected. If it stays wet, it makes a lot of wax and can harbour bacteria that can cause a smelly discharge. Dry the canal

with a twist of cotton-wool. Clean only the part of the ear that you can see. Do not poke anything rigid (such as a cotton bud) into the ear canal.

Q. When should I take her to see the health centre nurse?
A. First babies should probably go once a week to start with, until weight gain is established, then as often as you wish. For subsequent babies, fortnightly visits are usually enough.

Q. If my baby gets a rash, should I go on bathing her, and with what?
A. Don't use soap on the affected area. Use a non-soap cleanser or pine tar solution in her bath. It's not necessary to bathe her every day. First babies get bathed every day, second babies alternate days and fourth babies twice a week if they're lucky!

Q. How do I know when my baby has had enough at a feed?
A. She will stop sucking and may fall asleep (but not necessarily). If she does, don't wake her by burping her – put her down in her cot.

Q. How many wet nappies should I expect my baby to have each day?
A. Babies who are being well fed may have between five and twelve wet nappies a day. If she has only two, let your doctor or midwife know.

Q. How do I handle the stump of her umbilical cord? Will it bleed? When and how will it heal up and fall off?
A. Remember that your baby cannot feel pain from her umbilical cord (remember, we cut it with scissors at birth!) so handling it will cause her no discomfort. Give it a gentle tug when cleaning it to get down into the gutter. Cords often bleed a little in the days after birth, but it is usually only back-flow from the clotted veins within the cord, not blood from the baby. The umbilical cord heals up by becoming gummy and separating at the base. This process can take between four days and six weeks.

Q. Should I clean the baby's genital area? How? Should I draw back the foreskin or should I leave it alone?
A. BOYS: Do not draw back the foreskin until it has separated from the glans underneath; when it will become easier to retract. This may take a year or more. Take your lead from your little boy; he will play with it in his bath and show you how far back it can comfortably be retracted.
A. GIRLS: Gently spreading the outer lips and drawing a wet cotton-wool ball from front to back within the vulva is often necessary to clean it.

Disregard the advice frequently given that you should not wash in the vulva. The advice is meant to be 'don't poke anything into the vagina to clean it'. The vagina is self-cleaning.

Is my baby sick?

Suspecting that your baby is ill is as sickening a feeling as you can experience. Use the checklist here to see if the worry is justified or just normal overanxious parent syndrome! Trust your gut feelings, and if you're not sure, get her checked before darkness falls. At night everything looks worse – and you can't find a doctor without a three-hour wait.

Fevers, coughs and colds

It is unusual for newborn babies who are breastfed to get infections of the upper respiratory tract (coughs and colds) – there are antiviral substances in breastmilk that protect against them. Indeed, in the case of middle ear infection (otitis media), the effect of these substances seems to last even after the baby has been weaned and even if the breastfeeding only lasted a few weeks. That is not to say that the baby will not develop snuffles (see 'Snuffles').

Having said that, it is still possible for your baby to catch a cold, especially if the baby's older brother or sister is going to playgroup or preschool and bringing home all the viruses that are going around. If your baby has snuffles and a temperature, it is probably due to a viral infection. The normal underarm temperature for your baby is 36.5°C (97.7°F). Any temperature over 37°C (98.6°F) is probably significant. To take your baby's temperature, use a mercury or digital thermometer under her armpit or a stick-on one for her forehead.

If your baby has a cold, flu or a mild cough, just treat the symptoms. These illnesses are caused by viruses, and there are no antibiotics or drugs that can kill viruses. You have to wait for the baby's immune mechanism to fix the problem by itself.

◇ To control a high temperature between 37°C (98.6°F) and 38.3°C (101), a baby paracetamol elixir is very useful: give it in the correct dosage (15 mg/kg body weight) every four hours. This dosage must not be exceeded except with medical advice.

◇ Temperatures over 38.3 °C should definitely be treated with respect – take the baby to the doctor. If the baby has a viral illness, the temperature may stay high. We now know that high temperatures have a function, and that if they are left alone, the illnesses last slightly less long. However, the time difference is small, and if you would prefer to (and it may be more comfortable for the baby), you can give the baby paracetamol elixir regularly.

◇ If the baby has a blocked nose that is bad enough to interfere with feeding, a drop of saline (salt solution, as used for contact lens cleaning) or nasal antihistamine decongestant can clear it for long enough to get a feed down. It might be a good idea to have your doctor check to make sure there is no middle ear or chest infection.

Respiratory viral infections normally right themselves in a few days, but if your baby develops a wheeze, a seal-like bark or a 'smoker's cough', see your doctor straight away.

When to call the doctor

Babies have countless ways of worrying their parents, so it is important to remember that there is a great range of normal behaviour. All new parents are naturally anxious about their baby's health, and it is very easy to overreact.

However, if your baby exhibits any of the following signs or symptoms, get your doctor to check things out:

◇ baby's respiratory rate is 60 or more per minute maintained over five minutes or more

◇ baby's temperature is higher than 38.3°C (101°F) or below 36°C (96.8°F)

◇ fits or convulsions

◇ fewer than two wet nappies per day

◇ increasing jaundice beyond one week of age

◇ obvious blood in stool or urine beyond one week of age

◇ baby appears pale

◇ baby is drowsy and listless

◇ baby is floppy

◇ baby refuses feeds or takes less than half of normal over a few feeds

◇ combination of vomiting and watery diarrhoea
◇ repeated projectile vomiting
◇ any vomiting of bile
◇ symmetrical red inflammation around the base of the stump of the umbilical cord
◇ obvious generalised rash on trunk, or area of weeping rash bigger than 5 cm by 5 cm
◇ baby has difficulty breathing, with in-drawing of the chest
◇ baby has wheeze on breathing out (but not snuffles or upper respiratory noises)
◇ barking, 'seal-like' cough
◇ blue fingernails or toenails (beyond the first day after birth)
◇ unusual excessive crying
◇ baby does not move limbs symmetrically
◇ baby doesn't look right.

13

Colic and the crying baby

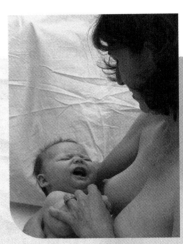

Hardly a parent exists who doesn't know what colic is, and judging by the responses on talkback radio, they all have a little theory about how to fix it. 'Try massaging the tummy (in a clockwise direction) with warm olive oil', or maybe 'put the baby, tummy down, over a rolling pin and move the gas along that way'. Poor parents. Poor baby.

All babies (even that perfect baby next door) exhibit some periods of unsettled behaviour in their first few weeks. Such irritability covers the full spectrum – from the majority, who have an unsettled period each evening, to those who cry the roof down for hours at a stretch.

Before leaping to diagnosis

Check the baby's weight – the little screamer might just be hungry. Sometimes it is difficult for breastfeeding mothers to get a feeling for how much the baby is taking in during the feeds. The system has actually been designed for her not to know, so the breast and the baby can regulate each other without interference. Occasionally, however, one can have the combination of a tolerant baby and a breast that underproduces. As the baby grows the situation deteriorates, and unsettledness begins.

Babies should put on at least 160 g a week. Most babies prefer about 180–200 g or more. If the baby is putting on less than this and is unsettled, all bets are off on colic diagnosis until the feeding issue is resolved. Talk to a lactation consultant – you may need to boost supply or consider complementary feeding if that fails.

Colic may be a secondary reason for unsettled behaviour, but hunger is the first thing that needs to be checked.

> Colic may be a secondary reason for unsettled behaviour; hunger is the first thing that needs to be checked.

A portrait of colic

At its worst, colic can drive families round the bend. The baby has prolonged periods of agonised screaming, drawing up his knees, screwing up his face and looking for all the world as if he has a terrible tummy-ache. These episodes are characteristically paroxysmal, and they wax and wane without apparent cause. The baby's movements are jerky and erratic, his stricken gaze darts about the room, his hands jerk and clasp at the air, and his screams cut the air like a knife.

It may start to build up during the afternoon to be in full voice by the evening; it can even wake the baby out of sleep with a jerk to herald hours of crying. Very soon the focus of the entire family is on finding the cause of his agony and fixing it. Often the search is futile; sometimes it even seems to make matters worse. However, Dad finds that the baby quietens if he is driven round in the car and Mum notices that he's better with the vacuum cleaner turned on nearby.

On reflection (hard to do with the baby screaming), it seemed he started after the relatives came to stay and he was handed around, or maybe after that lunch with the girls where they all admired him. Anyway, it was at around four weeks of age, soon after his smile appeared …

After a few weeks, with everyone in the family going mad, the marriage on the rocks, and the car out of petrol, the baby ends up in the hands of a professional. Not always a good move ...

Now the diagnoses start: 'colic', 'wind', 'reflux', 'lactose intolerance'. Each diagnosis has a treatment, each treatment is more complicated than the last, and anyway, none of them works.

In the end the beaten and demoralised parents, no longer breastfeeding, barely speaking to each other and desperate for sleep, give up hope for a quiet life.

And then the baby suddenly stops screaming. He's three months old now and sleeps like a baby. (It's often called 'three month colic'.)

Timing: 'evening' or 'three month' colic

This little scenario tends to start just before the baby starts to smile – at five to six weeks of age – and in many, it miraculously disappears at around three months. Why should this apparently physical complaint have such a specific timeframe? And why, for instance, does it start primarily in the evening (it's also called 'evening colic'), when the gut is active all the time? Why do babies who are fed breastmilk, the purest food on the planet, apparently suffer excruciating pain in their bowels? Why are babies temporarily improved by feeding, or soothing, or warm baths, but not by painkillers?

It's not tummy-ache

I was recently asked to speak at a large symposium on colic. There were about 20 speakers from every discipline that was involved in the 'screaming baby business': neonatologists, paediatricians, psychologists, psychiatrists, gastroenterologists, occupational therapists, physiotherapists ... they were all there. It was an interesting day as we all exchanged views about management to a large audience. However, the single most interesting thing for me was the fact that **not one speaker mentioned abdominal pain when discussing the cause of the baby's discomfort**. To this experienced group, it was a 'given' that whatever this syndrome is, it has nothing to do with the baby's tummy.

A scientific paper was once published referring to it as **C**ause **O**bscure, **L**engthy **I**nfant **C**rying, converting the word into an acronym to divert people from the intestinal aspects of the condition.

The answer is far simpler than tummy-ache, but it's subtle.

My husband found that the only way we could get the baby to stop crying was to load her in the car and drive her around. On one particularly bad night he drove round and round the block with her to shut her up. Unfortunately, he kept going past a speed camera. He got thirteen tickets. But we're appealing!

The cause of colic

To illustrate, let us step beyond three months, to when our screaming subject has recovered. He is now four months old.

He has slept well and he isn't hungry. He lies propped up on a pillow looking around. Suddenly he spies his mother across the room. His eyes light up and he starts to coo and wave his arms in an attempt to attract her. It doesn't take long. She stops what she's doing and her eyes meet those of her adorable baby. She is drawn to him as if she's on a string. She sits in front of him. Their gazes lock and they quickly become engrossed in each other. Conversation starts, mother warbling nonsense, baby replying in perfectly good baby sense. Their excitement rises, as their interaction becomes more intense.

Then, just as the conversation gets to a very exciting bit, the baby suddenly switches off, looks away, and shuts his mother out. He stares at his hands in his lap, his shoulders tense. After a moment, mother sees that his attention is elsewhere and she returns to what she was doing.

The baby sits stiffly in his chair. Gradually his shoulders relax as he calms himself. Time passes. He throws a quick glance at his mother, then looks away, looking back at his hands. Soon his glances to his mother become longer and longer as his body slowly relaxes. And it all starts again. He makes cooing noises, waves his arms and draws his mother back again. Attraction, rejection, attraction, rejection ... it follows an almost mechanically repeating loop.

What exactly is happening here?

The baby draws in his mother and their excitement rises as the stimulation of their interaction increases. The excitement then gets to a level that the baby starts to find uncomfortable, so he switches off and soothes himself. Cats do the same sort of thing – they break off from a fight and start washing to regain control of their emotional state and calm themselves down (it's called 'displacement activity').

So the baby gets more and more excited and more and more stimulated, until he can bear it no more. Then he shuts out the cause of stimulation and self-soothes. Babies figure this out at about three months of age. It's a developmental milestone, like smiling or walking. You can't learn to do it until you're ready.

At four weeks: the beginning of the problem

Why does colic usually start at four weeks? For the first four weeks the baby is mostly interested in warmth, breasts, milk, and mother. Then, about a week before he smiles, as the focal distance of his eyes increases he starts to look around and take in his environment. For the first time he starts giving attention to things around him. He is especially attracted to faces or eyes, and his gaze will follow them closely. He will start to watch the mobile above his cot and the curtain flapping by his window. When he does this, any adults in his vicinity (especially if it's his grandma!) will gaze back intensely, meeting his eyes. The baby's excitement level rises as he becomes stimulated by such things around him. The stimulation soon rises to a level that makes him uncomfortable, but alas, he has not yet developed the ability to self-soothe, and does not know how to deal with his increasing discomfort.

Dealing with discomfort

How do babies who are uncomfortable deal with it?

Crying

First, they cry. Crying is a de-stressor in humans and, as a technique for calming, it usually works well. However, in a baby's case this doesn't work so well, as it leads to increased attention and stimulation from his family. He's picked up, looked at closely and handed around, bounced and joggled – all this activity winds him up and makes matters worse, not better. The cry becomes a wail, as efforts to quieten him become even more frantic. He can't sleep because he's too excited, and he soon becomes overtired.

Tension

The baby's muscles tense. He starts to strain, push and groan. Soon he is taken to the doctor as he sounds as if he's constipated (even though the frequency and consistency of his stools are completely normal). Mother may even turn up at the doctor's surgery armed with a cassette player to play the sound of her baby's straining and groaning so somebody will believe the noise.

Comfort sucking

What else can a baby do? Well, he can suck. Sucking is a good way for babies to relax themselves, and this he knows. So he starts feeding, feeding, and feeding. From being a culturally acceptable six times a day feeder and sleeper, he rapidly develops into a half-hourly whingeing demander as he tries to use the breast as a soother. His weight balloons. But more important, the increased volume of feeds has a couple of other effects that confuse his carers.

1   More feeds equals more lactose. Soon he has so much lactose (the sugar in milk) that his small bowel can no longer absorb it all. The extra lactose escapes into the large bowel, which contains germs that act on it, fermenting it and producing volumes of hydrogen gas and lactic acid. The gas distends his bowel and he starts to produce numerous gassy explosive stools a day. He farts like a trooper. The lactic acid burns the skin on his bottom.

> The practice of burping babies is probably unnecessary. The valve between the oesophagus and stomach is so weak in the newborn, it can barely trap a feed, let alone an air bubble.

   Soon he is taken to the doctor. The doctor diagnoses lactose intolerance and suggests you stop breastfeeding and put him on a lactose-free formula. This is a seriously unhelpful.

2   More feeds mean that the stomach becomes very full. With a full stomach, our straining, pushing baby naturally vomits, vigorously and frequently.

   He is taken to the doctor, who diagnoses gastro-oesophageal reflux and may initiate hospital investigation before prescribing various medications, the least harmful of which is the antacid that he suggests should follow feeds.

3   'Wind'. Long before this, the parents have been told that their baby is 'windy'. They have been admonished for not burping the baby effectively and may even have been taught techniques to 'move the wind along'.

The truth of the matter is that crying babies swallow air. As a result, crying babies will often burp when picked up. But remember, it's the crying that causes the burping, not the other way around.

The practice of burping babies is probably completely unnecessary. The valve between the oesophagus and the stomach is so weak in the newborn that it can barely trap a feed, let alone an air bubble. After a feed babies just need to be cuddled and put down. If they want to burp they will do so in their own time.

More about 'wind'

Remember, the gas that comes out of the other end of the baby is hydrogen from the fermentation of lactose. It is mostly not swallowed air. If the baby does not release the air in the stomach with a burp, the air is absorbed into the baby's system. It does not pass along into the bowel to come out the other end.

The vicious cycles of colic

The colicky baby behaves as he does because he is caught in a set of vicious cycles:

◇ He's tense and overstimulated, then he gets overhandled. This makes him overfatigued and irritable, which keeps the cycle going.
◇ In an effort to help himself he initiates cycles of overfeeding, causing reflux vomiting and lactose spillage in his stools.

It is these downstream, secondary physical manifestations that occupy the attention of his carers – they often ignore the primary cause.

The answer

The situation can only be resolved by calming the baby down. Once the excessive stimulation is removed and the baby calms down, all the secondary effects will disappear of their own accord. Taking the baby into

The Colic Story

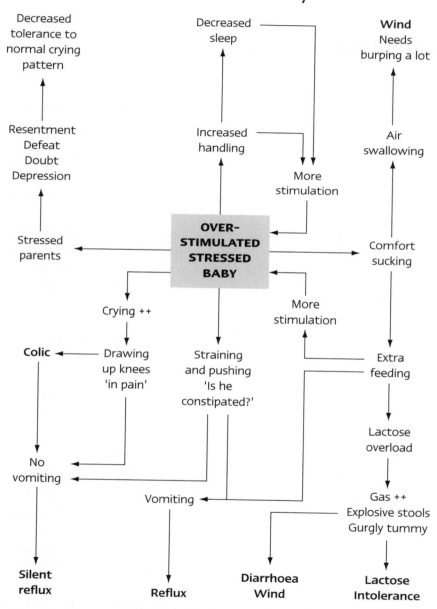

This chart shows the various vicious cycles you and your baby can get into when the 'colic syndrome' starts. The overstimulated, stressed baby cries excessively, so handling increases, which stimulates baby even more and around we go! The **bold** words are wrong diagnoses, made when the cycles are in full swing.

a quiet, neutral, unexciting environment for as long as it takes to calm him down will stop the vicious cycles.

Calming the baby

1   Send his grandparents home. If you have a toddler, send him with them.
2   Stick a note on the front door saying that you are out.
3   Go into his room, draw the blinds, and make the light in the room dim. Put on some quiet, restful music; that's for you, but babies do like a background of 'family sounds' rather than silence.
4   Get the baby and take him into the room with you. Do NOT leave him on his own.
5   Feed him on demand in the dim light, avoiding long periods of eye contact with him.
6   After the feed, wrap him firmly in a sheet. Wrap him with his back rounded and his limbs contained – this will remind him of the containment of the womb and help him feel secure. He may want to have his arms free, but it is preferable to contain them (see 'Wrapping your baby').
7   Place him in his cot, on his side, facing the wall. Pat him gently on the bottom at about 70 pats to the minute (mother's heart rate) and just …
8   BORE HIM TO SLEEP.
9   If it helps, give him a dummy.
10 If he gets upset (and he will), rewrap him and continue patting or feeding. If you're both going crazy, pick him up and cuddle him. Then put him in the cot again, on his side, and pat him again.
11 Continue this (hour after hour) until he settles. Do not leave the baby to cry, but you can leave the room when he finally sleeps.

Generally the first 24 hours are hell on wheels, but if you persevere, things will improve. He will eventually start to, as the psychologists say, 'return to base'.

By the second day he will be calmer. Do not take him out of the room, even though he seems improved. Give it another day, to be sure he loses some of his fatigue and stress.

The more he sleeps, the less opportunity there is for him to be stimulated, and the more he will sleep. This is a good cycle, not a vicious one. When he's calm and sleepy, you can return him to the living room.

You then need to keep the activity and stimulation in his environment down to a level that he can handle. How much stimulation your baby can cope with depends on his basic temperament. All babies are different. There are a few babies who self-soothe from the moment they're born. These babies can be taken to work and meet a hundred people and not get upset. Most babies have a limit, though – you need to find out where your baby's limit is and keep the level under that.

Premature babies and stimulation

Ex-premature babies are often very sensitive to their surroundings and need gentle handling, plus restriction of playtime and family interaction, perhaps because of their prolonged experience outside the womb in an immature state.

Some ex-premature babies are on such a hair-trigger that if you pick them up, look at them and to talk to them at the same time they will cry, backarch and withdraw. You can talk to them, or hold them or look at them – but you can't do those things simultaneously, and you can't do them very often.

'Christmas colic'

Too much activity, too many relatives and too many parties in late December means packed paediatric surgeries in early January – surgeries full of tense, screaming babies who can't wait for everybody to settle down and go home!

I recall on a couple of occasions stir-crazy mothers phoning me asking what to do. They were trapped in their houses with a baby who was quiet and calm in his room but who screamed and overloaded as soon as he went beyond the front gate. My advice was to buy their groceries online.

Having triplets has taught me more in a given period of time than anything else in my life, especially since my lessons were dependent on my children's wellbeing. I was blessed with two girls and a boy. My first lesson was that boys truly are different to girls, not only from my own experience but also from my observations of other children.

My little boy, named Joshua, needed more attention than the girls from day one. He slept his soundest when the girls were sleeping beside him and often woke up if he was left on his own. This was not the case with my two very independent girls.

An interesting experience I had was the apparent 'anxiety attacks' Joshua started to develop around the same time he was starting to see things. The children were all on four-hourly feeds – firstly breastfed, then bottle-fed with formula. Feeding time was never a problem, with each one feeding for approximately twenty minutes. As the weeks progressed and Joshua became more visual, feeding *him* started to become a major problem. I sensed that as he began to see new things every day, he became 'overwhelmed' to the point of no longer being able to feed despite his healthy appetite. I knew it wasn't colic or reflux (as friends and family can be quick to advise).

Then I received some sound advice to simply feed him in the dark – but there was no room dark enough in my house to feed Joshua, besides for the evening feeds. I felt isolated from family and friends who came around to help. I began to blindfold him, which was an absolute turning point for both Joshua and I. Initially I used a thin cotton baby wrap to cover his eyes, but as he became more mobile it became a struggle to keep it on. Eventually my husband suggested using a proper blindfold, like on international plane trips. This worked perfectly: Joshua fed well every time, and because he was used to it from very early on, he just accepted it.

Joshua stopped having to wear his blindfold just before he turned five months old. He is now a gorgeous, thriving two-year-old toddler.

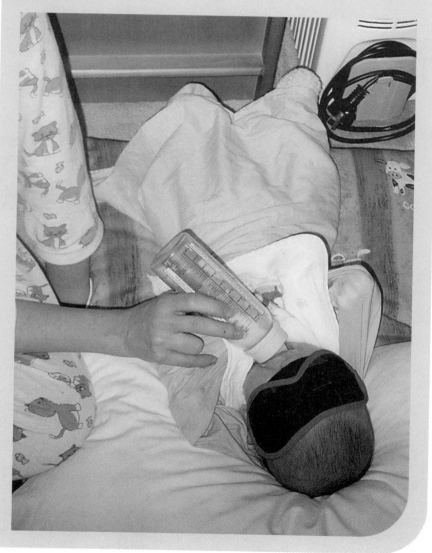

14

Immunisation

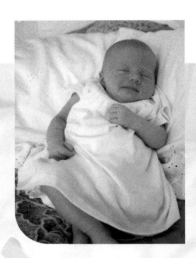

Immunisation is one of the greatest gifts of medical science.

It's very hard to believe that there are still people around who believe the world is flat. You can show them maps, even pictures from space, but they still go on believing their nonsense. It is a similar story with immunisation. There are people who never waste an opportunity to push their belief that immunisation is useless, even harmful. The media are often to blame – they invariably sensationalise any tragedy that relates to immunisation and inappropriately lay blame. This only reinforces the biases of the ignorant.

The anti-immunisation lobby bases much of its argument on the fact that in the West, infectious diseases were generally on the wane before the introduction of immunisation. This was usually because of improvements in hygiene, sanitation and nutrition. However, immunisation programs had an enormous impact, independent of these environmental improvements.

Make no mistake. There is an overwhelming and vast body of evidence that shows that immunisation works.

Look at the logic. In order to believe the anti-immunisation people, you have to believe that there is a massive conspiracy of literally tens of thousands – maybe hundreds of thousands – of doctors and other medical staff. These paediatricians, infectious disease specialists and immunologists are apparently prepared to put the world's babies at risk because they are beholden to a global medico-industrial conglomerate, or perhaps because they are all simultaneously misled by their equally deluded research and epidemiological peers.

More likely, the anti-immunisation lobby has a primary distrust (or lack of understanding) of things scientific or statistical. For instance, if you were told that of new cases of Disease A, half were people who were immunised, you might think that it is hardly worth immunising for Disease A (this argument is frequently used). Let us say that immunisation for Disease A had an effectiveness of 90 percent and an uptake in the community of 90 percent.

Think about it: the 10 percent of the child population who are not immunised get the disease, and the other 10 percent of the child population who get it are immunised but are still vulnerable. Half-and-half. It doesn't mean the immunisation doesn't work. You have to look at the attack rates. *All* the unimmunised children get the disease but only one out of ten of those who were vaccinated get it. The reason it comes out half–half is because there were more people who were immunised to start with. There are still *far* fewer cases of the disease than there would have been if we didn't immunise at all.

Anti-immunisation people frequently rely too heavily on anecdote. Take the idea that the incidence of SIDS rose after immunisation, which was widely believed for a while. Careful studies showed that the incidence was actually *lower*, but with the peak incidence of cot death occurring around the time when immunisations began, it is not surprising that such coincidences occur. The same goes for the MMR vaccine and the incidence of autism (see pages 160–161). Cases of autism don't come to attention until after the child is a year old, so of course there will be children who apparently present with autism symptoms after having had the vaccine. And when this happens, it's an understandable relief for the parents to find something they can blame rather than seeing the autism as just a terrible piece of bad luck. Unfortunately, the two things just aren't related through cause and effect.

This chapter will outline all the individual immunisations your baby needs and look at the evidence that makes doctors, nurses, public health officials (and most parents) very enthusiastic about immunisation being available for every baby.

How does immunisation work?

The aim of immunisation is to protect the body from viral and bacterial organisms (germs) and the poisons (toxins) they produce when they enter the body. This is achieved by giving the body a tiny dose of killed, or altered germ, or inactivated toxin (toxoid). This tiny dose of the germ makes the body produce an antibody (that is, a neutralising agent) that fights infection by that germ. By teaching the body to produce the appropriate antibody in advance of invasion by the germ we can get it to develop a solid defence against the disease those germs produce. The germ never gets started. As they enter the body the germs are overwhelmed and removed by our defence mechanisms.

'Passive immunisation' from maternal antibodies

At birth, babies have the same antibodies as their mother – these have been transported to them across the placenta. If the mother is immune to chickenpox or measles or tetanus, through having had either the disease or the immunisation, then so is her baby. This is called passive immunisation, and it lasts from three to six months for most diseases. After this, the level of antibodies in the baby falls very low, and she is no longer protected. At this time the baby needs the active immunisation that is the subject of this chapter.

The triple/hep B/polio vaccine

This vaccine is, in full, the DTPa (triple antigen) vaccine combined with the hepatitis B vaccine (Infanrix-hepb) and the Sabin vaccine. At eight weeks your baby should have the first in a series of three triple vaccine injections – these will prevent her getting diphtheria, tetanus and pertussis (whooping cough), and hepatitis B. She will also be given an oral vaccine, the Sabin vaccine, to prevent her getting poliomyelitis. These vaccines will be given at two months, four months and six months. At eighteen months she should have just the triple, without the polio or HIB – the timing of this last one varies somewhat from country to country.

Diphtheria

In the past this was a real killer: in the 1880s it carried off about 14 percent of toddlers in South Australia. In 1890 passive immunisation, with an injection of the antibody to the germ's toxin (taken from people who had had the disease), reduced the incidence by 50 percent. Even so, just before World War II, 300 people each year were still dying from the disease in Australia. Soon after that, active immunisation with the diphtheria toxoid was introduced, and the disease all but disappeared.

The germ of diphtheria lives in the soil and dust and can infect the skin directly. However, the more common form is a severe throat infection, spread by contact with the droplets in a cough or a sneeze. The toxin produced by the germ can cause death by suffocation or (more commonly) by heart failure.

Tetanus

Tetanus is another extremely nasty disease lurking out there. The spores of the disease are common in our environment, ready to pounce on us if we drop our guard. Tetanus is an often fatal disease caused by the toxin produced by the tetanus bacillus. This germ gets into deep tissues, usually through a penetrating (but often very small) wound in our skin. The toxin causes muscle spasms and organ failure.

Tetanus is still a common cause of death of babies in the Third World, where the organism gets access through the umbilical cord (occasionally

from tribal customs such as putting animal dung on the umbilical stump).
Many babies in developing countries are now being saved by active
immunisation of the mother, whose antibodies are then transferred to the
baby through the placenta during the last few weeks of pregnancy.

Tetanus immunisation works very well for the individual who is
immunised, and lasts a long time. However, unlike the situation with
contagious diseases, the risk of disease in unimmunised individuals is not
affected by the high level of immunisation in the community. Tetanus
immunisation is entirely our own and our children's responsibility.

Remember, every unimmunised person can catch and be killed by
tetanus from a dirty cut – any time, anywhere. Unimmunised people here
are as vulnerable as people in undeveloped nations that can't get the
immunisation. And remember, our antibody level needs to be raised
regularly – we all need a booster immunisation every ten years.

Pertussis

Pertussis (whooping cough) is a respiratory tract infection characterised by
paroxysms of fitful coughing and the production of sticky, gluey mucus. The
cough empties the lungs of air so much that, in children, after the coughing
spasm there is a 'whoop' (pronounced 'hoop') as air is sucked back into the
lungs. It is a serious and prolonged illness in children (in China it is
called the 'hundred-day cough'), and is common in adults, but it actually
kills babies.

This is because they often have the disease without the characteristic
cough – they have attacks where they just stop breathing. There has been
a recent resurgence of this disease despite good vaccination rates in the
population. This is probably because of a large reservoir of the bacteria in
the adult population – up to a quarter of the infants who get it catch it from
an adult in their household who has a cough. It is the unimmunised babies
in the population who pay the price for whooping cough germs out there,
though, with one in 200 of the babies who catch it dying from pneumonia
or brain damage. Babies can't be immunised until they are two months old
(it doesn't 'take' before then), so to protect them we must reduce the
amount of this germ in the population by immunisation.

The newer acellular vaccine consists of parts of the germ and germ
toxin that stimulate antibody formation. It is effective in about 90 percent
of cases. This is enough to prevent the spread of infection. In public health

jargon, it improves 'herd immunity', that is, it reduces the number of people who are harbouring the germ at any time and therefore reduces the opportunity of spreading it to others who are vulnerable, such as babies.

The older vaccine

The older vaccine was, unfortunately, not universally accepted, despite being a safe, effective vaccine. It was this component of the triple vaccine that caused most of the vaccine's side effects, and this vaccine that led to the incorrect belief that vaccination can cause permanent brain or neurological damage. In the vaccination tragedies that hit the papers, it was usually the pertussis vaccine that was to blame.

In the United Kingdom before the 1950s there were about 100,000 notified cases of pertussis each year, with numerous deaths. By 1973, following the introduction of a vaccination program, 80 percent of the population had been vaccinated and the number of cases had dropped to a little over 2000 a year.

> An unimmunised person can be killed by tetanus from a dirty cut – any time, anywhere.

Then two things happened. First, people started to think that whooping cough had been defeated, and they stopped fearing the disease. Second, publicity about the side effects of the immunisation started to appear more often.

Consequently, immunisation rates fell, and by 1975 only 30 percent of the population were immune. The country paid the price. In 1978 and 1982 there were epidemics, each of which had over 65,000 cases and about 30 deaths.

There were similar experiences in Sweden and Japan.

The results of non-immunisation

The pertussis immunisation story demonstrates graphically the most powerful arguments against those who would not immunise.

Nobody could argue that improvements in environmental conditions, general nutrition or hygiene (the usual reasons given by anti-immunisation groups to explain falling disease rates) were relevant to the impact of the immunisation program.

The epidemics were solely a result of the increase in the number of children who were at risk of getting the infection (that is, a fall in herd immunity). This was a direct result of complacency, scaremongering, and the fear of what are, in fact, minimal side effects.

Side effects

A few babies will suffer some side effects from pertussis immunisation. Usually this is only a small local reaction – a red weal or swelling at the site of the injection. Babies may also get a mild fever or be a bit whingey for a few hours. Paracetamol will relieve these symptoms: give 15 mg/kg at the time of the injection and every four hours (if the baby is awake) for three or four doses.

A small percentage of children will have side effects that are a bit more worrying. Two percent of children may get a fever over 38°C, and some children may cry for more than three hours or lose their appetite. Very occasionally a baby will have a hypotonic/ hyporesponsiveness episode: the baby becomes floppy and apparently unconscious. Even more rarely a baby can get shock reactions and even brain swelling. None of these reactions, frightening though the rare ones are, causes permanent damage. All resolve without problems to the baby.

As most babies are immunised, it is likely that some babies will have unrelated problems – such as fits or even cot death – at around the same time. When this happens, one can't blame parents for looking for a previous event to be the cause, and therefore believing that the pertussis vaccine caused the problem. However, blaming the pertussis vaccine has been shown, by the most exhaustive and extensive studies, to be completely unwarranted.

Research

The National Collaborative Perinatal Project (USA) investigated the incidence of fits following the older (and more reaction-prone) type of immunisation. It found that by chance alone two out of every 10,000 children would have a fit within two days of any given time. They then studied the two days following the immunisation, and found that only 1.5 children per 10,000 actually had a seizure. Therefore, if it happened, it was coincidence.

An even more detailed study, the National Childhood Encephalopathy Study (UK) looked at the incidence of permanent brain disorders following immunisation. It came to a provisional (and much publicised) conclusion that the chance was 'less than one in 310,000', but since the original publication the data has been re-examined in even greater detail, and the present estimation is that the risk is 'virtually zero'.

In conclusion

To sum up, if a baby is diagnosed as having a neurological problem that becomes apparent only after an immunisation, it is easy for a journalist to write an emotive story which blames the pertussis immunisation and plucks at the heartstrings. But the scientists who have researched this area have found no relationship between the pertussis vaccine and permanent neurological disorders.

The same can be said for the relationship between immunisation and cot death. By its very nature, cot death leaves parents and their friends looking for a cause, and if the baby had been immunised in the previous few days, it is easy to understand that they might blame the immunisation – but it is incorrect. There is no relationship, no connection, between the two. Let us hope that unbalanced media coverage and the scaremongering of the pressure groups are not too influential, because if these things reduce immunisation rates, there will be an increase in the number of young babies dying from such diseases.

> Breastfeeding does not affect the oral polio vaccine.

Poliomyelitis

This was one of the few diseases that became *more* common when living conditions improved in the developed world: if poliomyelitis is contracted by a very young child, as happens in underdeveloped countries, it usually causes no problems. However, when it is acquired for the first time later in childhood or in early adult life, it can lead to paralysis. During the 1940s and 1950s there were epidemics in the West, and in Australia there was widespread panic, as the disease led to an average of 100 deaths per year.

Poliomyelitis is a gut infection caused by viruses that then invade the nervous system. It is passed from person to person by bad hygiene or poor sanitation. The first vaccine developed was called the Salk vaccine; it was made from killed polioviruses which, when injected, caused the formation of antibodies. This vaccine cut the disease rate by 99 percent after the first year of introduction.

Later the Sabin vaccine was introduced. This was an oral vaccine (taken by mouth, not by injection like the Salk). Mass immunisation programs were started and the disease was virtually eliminated from the developed world. The Sabin vaccine contains strains of living polioviruses that have been 'attenuated', or made weaker. After a person takes the vaccine, the virus establishes itself in the bowel, and causes the formation of antibodies in the lining of the bowel and in the blood, thus preventing later infection by the infective type of virus. It works very well – many babies are immune after their first dose. A full course of three doses will produce lifelong immunity in more than 95 percent of people.

Polio vaccines and immunity

A word of caution. Oral polio vaccine is extremely safe, but if the recipient's immunity is not working efficiently, for any reason, the vaccine should not be given. It should not be given to:

⬦ those receiving immunosuppressive drugs (including radiation);
⬦ those receiving corticosteroids (except as cream on the skin);
⬦ those suffering from lymphoma, leukaemia or tumours of the immune system.

The Salk vaccine should be used for these patients instead. The Salk vaccine should also be used for babies who are going to be living in households where there are people with the above conditions, as the viruses could be passed on to them. It is likely that the Salk vaccine will make a comeback into the routine immunisation schedule in the near future.

Breastfeeding does not affect the oral polio vaccine.

Hepatitis B

This virus causes liver disease and is common worldwide. Older children (non-newborns) and adults who get it suffer acute liver inflammation, and about 5 percent of these people become long-term carriers of the virus. Infected infants rarely get the acute form of hepatitis, but most of them become carriers. Carriers are a danger to others because they are a source of the virus, and to themselves because they have an increased risk of chronic liver disease or liver cancer. Exposure to blood and other body secretions (especially sexual) from an infected person can transmit the virus.

The most common transmission of this virus globally is from mothers who are carriers of the disease to their babies, around the time of delivery. These babies need to be immunised at birth to prevent them becoming carriers and so perpetuating the disease. It is rare for babies and children to catch hepatitis B 'horizontally' (from other adults or children with whom they play or live), but immunisation is still strongly recommended. The disease becomes a danger later, when sexual activity begins, or if intravenous drug-taking starts. So make sure your adolescent children are immunised well before the age of sex, drugs and rock'n'roll – at twelve years old, perhaps.

In order to control the spread of the disease generally, and to protect younger children against the possibility of, for instance, a needle-stick injury from an addict's syringe on the beach, the vaccine is now part of the routine immunisation program for all children. The vaccine is completely safe, and is combined with the triple vaccine given at two, four and six months. We all need a Hep B booster vaccination every ten years to stay immunised.

To vaccinate or not to vaccinate?

It is **okay** to vaccinate if:

◇ There was a local reaction from the previous dose but it was less than 5 cm across.
◇ The baby had a fever after the last dose of less than 40.5°C (104.9°F).
◇ The baby has recently been exposed to, or convalesced from, an infectious disease.
◇ The baby has had a mild infective illness.
◇ The baby is currently on antibiotic therapy.
◇ The child's mother (or someone else in the household) is pregnant.
◇ The baby's family has a history of convulsions, or sudden infant death syndrome. Also, if the family has a history of significant adverse events after immunisation.
◇ The baby has a static neurological disease (such as cerebral palsy) or a progressive neurological disease. Naturally, check with your doctor. The reason such diseases have been contraindications in the past is the fear of the normal progression of the disease being blamed on the immunisation.
◇ The baby was premature. Premature babies should be vaccinated according to their chronological age – counting from the time they were born – because their immunity starts to mature as soon as they are born.

Don't vaccinate if after the previous immunisation the baby had:

◇ convulsions
◇ encephalopathy (swelling of the brain), even though this condition invariably gets better
◇ persistent screaming for three hours
◇ collapse or a shock-like state
◇ a fever greater than 40.5°C

Contraindications to vaccination

A study from Sydney showed that 16 percent of children seen in a children's hospital casualty department were over a month late for their vaccinations. This happens because many people want their babies and children to be in perfect physical health before they are immunised, so they will delay immunisation for even a cough, sniffle or minor temperature. This is not in the best interests of the baby. In fact there are very few true contraindications to vaccination – unless the baby has a real illness or is obviously actively fighting an infection (if she has a high fever), she should have her immunisations on time.

Haemophilus influenzae type B (HIB)

Tears of joy stung the paediatric community's eyes on the release of a vaccine that really works against HIB disease. This nasty little bug was the commonest life-threatening bacterial infection in Australian children between the ages of one month and five years. It caused invasive infection in one in about 300 children. Of these children, about 20 died each year in Australia and an equal number were left with a severe handicap.

◇ **Children under the age of two**: in this age group, HIB tended to cause meningitis, which could kill or cause brain damage. There used to be a particularly high incidence in the Aboriginal community in babies under six months of age.
◇ **Children between two and five years old**: as they got older this germ gave them a disease called epiglottitis (to which they were not immune even if they had had the HIB meningitis). In this disease there is

extreme swelling of the soft tissues at the top of the throat, which causes respiratory obstruction, asphyxia and death unless the child receives intensive care quickly. Children can also get infections of the skin, joints and bones.

This disease is, we hope, starting to become rare in the countries that have immunisation programs. There are several so-called conjugate vaccines against HIB available and they are all effective; however, babies require at least three doses of any HIB vaccine in the first twelve months to become immune.

This is another of those infections where herd immunity is important, as there is a reservoir of this germ in our community, mostly in the under-fives themselves. In the US this disease is called the 'day care' disease – the more children a small child meets, the more likely she is to meet someone with the germ. Some countries, such as Finland, have completely eliminated the disease, even though not everybody has been immunised, by building up enough herd immunity and gradually eliminating the reservoirs.

These vaccines also cause very little in the way of side effects, either local or general. They are combined with the triple/hep B immunisation at two and four months, and need a booster at twelve months to complete the course.

Measles, mumps and rubella (MMR)

At twelve to fifteen months your baby will be due for her measles, mumps and rubella immunisation. In some countries they give it earlier – at nine months – and then give a booster later.

Measles

Measles is a highly infectious disease. During the infectious stage, which lasts three weeks, vast numbers of viral particles are excreted in the respiratory secretions, and these have a high likelihood of infecting any unimmunised person. So even with high immunisation rates in the population, epidemics can still occur.

For those who are immunised, the vaccine is very effective: in the US, for example, the number of measles cases was reduced from 3.3 million to 3500 per year by an immunisation program in the early 1980s.

If your baby is exposed to measles before being immunised, make sure she gets immunised immediately. This, plus the antibody given her from the placenta at birth, will give her adequate protection.

Measles is not a trivial disease. In the Third World it causes over 1.5 million deaths each year, and even in developed countries there can be neurological and respiratory complications that cause handicap and death.

Mumps

Mumps is less contagious than measles, and it generally infects older children and adults. Nevertheless, it is the commonest viral infection of the nervous system, with 15 percent of mumps sufferers having signs of meningitis such as severe headache or neck stiffness. Luckily, sufferers usually completely recover from these symptoms. It also often causes inflammation of the testicles and infertility in postpubertal males.

Immunisation works very well. In the US between 1967 and 1983 there was a 98 percent decrease in notifications following a vaccination program.

Rubella

Rubella (German measles) is a relatively minor infectious disease, which causes fever and a mild rash in most people. Its effect on the foetus, however, can be terrible: rubella damages the foetus and causes congenital malformations if the mother catches it during the first three months of her pregnancy.

In the past, only young teenage girls were vaccinated – this still left a lot of virus among young males, so any woman whose immunity was not complete could still be infected.

Immunisation programs are extremely effective but we need to achieve as near to 100 percent compliance as possible, to remove the reservoir of virus in the population, and so totally eliminate this disease.

MMR (Measles Mumps, Rubella) vaccine and autism

Recently there was a major splash in the media about this vaccine possibly being related to autism. This caused a very careful and thorough re-examination of all the information by experts from around the world. All the panels agree that there is no relationship, other than coincidence.

We administer these immunising agents to all the healthy children in the community. Of course the most important thing is that these agents do no harm. If it were ever proved – or even suspected – that they do harm, doctors would immediately put a hold on administering them.

When to vaccinate

The vaccine for measles, mumps and rubella is a mixture of live attenuated (inactivated) viruses. The vaccine should be administered at twelve months of age and again in the early teenage years. There are, however, some contraindications.

Contraindications to the MMR vaccine

◇ Severe infective illness.
◇ Hypersensitivity to neomycin or kanamycin. If your child is allergic to eggs it doesn't mean she cannot have the vaccine; it means the vaccination should be done under medical supervision.
◇ Previous anaphylactic (severe allergic) reaction.
◇ Impaired immunity.
◇ Pregnancy.
◇ An injection of immunoglobulin or blood transfusion in the previous three months.

Other newer vaccines

There have been a number of new vaccines introduced lately. These have not yet entered the routine list, either because they are very expensive and the diseases they prevent are not so common, or because they are only effective against a few strains of the germs causing the disease. However, as they are so effective, we can expect them to join the immunisation schedule soon.

Chickenpox vaccine

This is a seriously good vaccine that should turn the tide on a common and potentially nasty disease. Most people think that it's just an inconvenient illness of a few spots for a few days. Not so. Especially in the under-15s, chickenpox can cause disease that needs hospitalisation and 10 percent of these cases are for serious complications like pneumonia or brain swelling.

The vaccine is really effective in children and protects 98 percent of recipients after a single dose (adults need two doses). The few who get chickenpox after vaccination get a very mild form of it. The vaccine has only a few, and minor, side effects, and the antibody appears to last for a long time (a Japanese study showed the antibody still there after 20 years).

When to vaccinate

Nine months–twelve years: one dose.
Adolescents and adults: two doses, six to eight weeks apart.

Pneumococcal vaccine

This germ (*Streptococcus pneumoniae*) causes various forms of invasive disease – pneumonia, middle ear infection or meningitis, for example – in young children. There are over 80 different strains of the germ; the vaccine is effective against the seven most important strains – they cover over 80 percent of the cases of severe illness. The vaccine is close to 100 percent effective against them. It has also resulted in major reduction in disease from the other strains, so it is well worth getting.

In Australia it is free for all Aboriginal children under two years (whose incidence of the disease is high), and for Aboriginal children up to five years in Central Australia and those with special risk factors (such as reduced immunity). It can be bought by everyone else on request.

When to vaccinate

Two, four and six months, or up to two years of age. Up to five years if high risk.

Meningococcal disease

I am happy to report that this terrible disease is not as common as you might think from picking up the newspaper. It tends to strike down teenagers with frightening speed, and cause immense grief and tragedy to the victims and their families, but, luckily, population-wide it is quite rare. The disease primarily results in infection of the blood (septicaemia) or meningitis (inflammation of the membranes around the brain and spinal cord), and is caused by the bacterium *Neisseria meningitidis*. The infection is very serious, and can rapidly cause loss of life or limb.

There are various strains of the germ – types A, B, C Y and W_{135} are the ones that cause most of the illness. Type B is the most common (with about a 6 percent death rate); type C is slightly less common, but has a death rate of 12 percent.

The age group most at risk is the 15–24 year group, but the babyhood to four-years group is also at risk. The incidence of disease is around four to six cases per 100,000, but up to 20 percent of the population can be symptomless carriers (mostly they carry the disease in the throat or nose). Once there is a single case, secondary cases (people who have been in contact with the first case) can occur between two and five days later. Giving these people an antibiotic (rifapicin) should prevent secondary cases.

Vaccines

◇ There is an older vaccine (the 'polysaccharide') that worked against types A, C, Y and W. It didn't work at all in children under two years and even in older kids the antibody level didn't last long, and with repeated doses the body made less and less antibody.

◇ The latest vaccine is much more effective, but only against type C. However, this is the most lethal type. This vaccine works in all age groups and can be given to babies from six weeks of age. Babies tolerate the vaccine well, and there are few side effects (no serious ones). The trouble is, the vaccine costs about $70 per dose, and as the disease is relatively rare, it is not cost effective to put it in the regular immunisation routine for everyone. My advice is, if you can, buy it!

When to vaccinate

From six weeks: three doses with a month between doses.

Immunisation schedule

AGE	IMMUNISATION
AT BIRTH	Hep B
2 MONTHS	First dose of DTPa (triple antigen), Hep B, HIB vaccine and Sabin (polio) vaccine. Pneumococcal vaccine for Aboriginal or Torres Strait Islander (ATSI) infants.
4 MONTHS	Second dose of DTPa (triple antigen), Hep B, HIB vaccine and Sabin (polio) vaccine. Pneumococcal vaccine for ATSI infants.
6 MONTHS	Third dose of DTPa (triple antigen), Hep B and Sabin (polio) vaccine. Pneumococcal vaccine for ATSI infants.
12 MONTHS	Measles, mumps and rubella vaccine (MMR). HIB vaccine.
18 MONTHS	Fourth dose of DTPa (triple antigen).
4 YEARS	Pre-school booster – DTPa (triple antigen), MMR, and Sabin (polio) vaccine.
IMMUNISATION RECORDS	◇ Record all your baby's immunisations in the Personal Health Record, sometimes known as the 'blue book'. ◇ Accurate immunisation records will make it easy for your child to get an immunisation certificate when she starts school.

Homeopathic immunisation

There is absolutely no scientific evidence that so-called homeopathic immunisation bestows anything except a false sense of security.

The circumcision decision

Most of us know that circumcision is an ancient Jewish ritual dating back to the time of Abraham, but few of us realise that the Jews were not the first to practise it. Carvings on the walls in the Temple of Karnak depict Egyptian priests over 6000 years ago performing circumcision, making it probably the oldest surgical operation known. Many diverse cultures continue the practice today.

In modern times circumcision became extremely popular between the two world wars – especially in the USA and Australia (rather less in the UK). The influential American paediatrician, Benjamin Spock, though not wholly recommending it, thought that 'it made a boy feel regular', as virtually all boys in that era were circumcised.

But times are changing. Nowadays, in city obstetric hospitals over 70 percent of male babies are going home with their foreskin – often to the dismay of their grandparents.

Circumcision is an ancient practice, so it is not surprising that numerous myths have sprung up about it. Circumcision 'weakens the penis' and therefore limits intercourse (so said a twelfth century rabbi); increases (others say decreases) sexual pleasure; decreases sexual desire; prolongs the ability to have intercourse (in the act and in life); makes men better warriors and better husbands; reduces masturbation; and cures bed-wetting. These claims are difficult to research, as you can imagine, but all are unreasonable and defy common sense.

We like to think we are more reasonable in our beliefs now. However, the procedure continues to have vocal advocates and critics both within medicine and without. Professors of urology argue with paediatricians, family doctors in the cities argue with those in the bush, surgeons argue with psychiatrists. Outside medicine the discussion gets even hotter among action groups such as the American NOCIRC (National Organisation of Circumcision Resource Centers) and INTACT (International Organisation Against Circumcision Trauma), both of which have members who have undergone plastic surgery to reconstruct the foreskin and psychotherapy to relieve the psychological stress suffered by its removal.

The essence of the discussion remains simple. Does the latest information on the subject justify routine circumcision on babies? For other invasive baby routines, such as immunisation or the administration of vitamin K, the benefits are so overwhelming and the risk so small that there's no need for discussion. Circumcision, however, is another matter. The question is, should we routinely subject a baby – or any minor who can't give his personal consent – to a procedure whose benefits are not proven or substantial, and whose risk is not negligible, and which involves removing a piece of his body whose function is not clear?

The function of the foreskin

Logically, it seems likely that the foreskin has some function. Most of our other useless organs have been discarded by the process of evolution or remain only in a shrunken, vestigial form. Not so with the foreskin, which remains as large as life. Microscopic examination of the cells on the inside of the foreskin shows that it contains many sensory nerve endings relating to sexual excitation. In addition, the nerves on the outside of the foreskin are numerous and similar to normal skin – hence they can discriminate fine touch, texture and warmth, and they can stretch. Not so the skin of the tip of the penis – this is relatively insensitive to warmth, touch and texture.

It would seem reasonable, if the foreskin were being removed for social reasons, to obtain the permission of the owner. At the age of 20 he should be able to make an informed decision. Moreover, it is totally wrong to suggest that circumcision hurts more at that age. In fact it is not a particularly painful operation – as long as one has a general anaesthetic and there is no postoperative arousal!

It is certainly an advantage for a newborn to keep his foreskin. It protects the penile tip or glans from the effects of nappy rash and will prevent the formation of meatal ulceration, a small painful ulcer that develops at the opening of the urethra only in the circumcised.

Another common reason given for circumcision of the newborn is that the foreskin causes urinary obstruction. This is almost never the case – if it occurs at all it must be incredibly rare. Certainly, there is often ballooning of the foreskin on passing urine, but this is certainly not an indication for its removal either.

When the foreskin draws back

A common reason given for circumcision in a baby is phimosis, or narrowing of the foreskin. Many people – including many medical and nursing professionals, sadly – are not aware that in the majority of baby boys the foreskin is not retractable. Only in 4 percent of newborns can the foreskin be fully retracted. As time passes the foreskin gradually separates from the underlying tissue, but even at three years of age there are 10 percent of boys whose foreskin cannot be retracted. In these boys, as there is no space between the foreskin and the glans, no secretions collect, so there is no need for this area to be washed.

After the foreskin becomes retractable, such secretions do tend to accumulate and regular hygiene is necessary each bathtime. Many misguided people forcibly retract the foreskin of the infant before it is ready – this causes tearing of the tissues, which leads to scarring and the possibility of narrowing (phimosis). All this then makes retraction and normal hygiene extremely difficult. In fact, to correct this situation, circumcision may subsequently be required. Most people who recommend circumcision have gruesome tales of close friends or relations who had 'years of infection, pain and worry' from a foreskin that was too narrow until they were liberated by circumcision. One wonders how many of these poor men were suffering from a consequence of obsessive early retraction and penile cleansing when things would have been better left alone.

Medical studies

Some medical studies, however, have provided a bit more balance to the circumcision argument. First, a study of the medical records of babies born in US Army hospitals has shown an increased incidence of urinary tract infection in the first few years of life in those who were uncircumcised. The incidence of infection was still very small (about one in 600 babies), but it was ten times the rate for the circumcised. There remain some theoretical criticisms of the study, so the conclusion is not yet proven, but as other similar studies seem to have arrived at the same conclusion, it is likely to be true.

It is still debatable that the possibility of urinary tract infection justifies the routine circumcision of every baby; for instance, the incidence of appendicitis is about the same (one in 700 per year) but we do not recommend routine appendicectomy. Certainly this newer information has not changed the stance of the American Pediatric Association, which is still against routine circumcision.

The second study concerned sexually transmitted organisms. During sexual activity there is always the possibility of small breaks occurring in the foreskin when it is stretched around the glans. These breaks can make it easier for some viral organisms (such as herpes, warts and HIV) to enter the body. It has been claimed that having unprotected intercourse with an HIV-positive person is eight times more risky if one is uncircumcised than if one is circumcised. This sounds logical and reasonable. Under that circumstance circumcision sounds a worthwhile thing to do. Using a condom would also be a sensible thing to do.

It also seems to be true that cancer of the penis hardly occurs in the circumcised. But the incidence (less than one per 100,000, which is really rare) seems to be the same in the uncircumcised who wash themselves. Again, not a powerful argument unless your family are congenitally lazy in the bathroom!

The parents' decision

Far and away the most common reason for circumcision in the newborn period is parental preference. Parents often believe that it is the 'normal thing to do'. A father often wishes his son to be 'done' so that his penis and his son's penis look the same, lest any differences cause the boy upset and confusion. Children accept differences with far greater equanimity than adults, though, and the major difference between father and son – penile size – remains until the boy is well into puberty anyway. If the boy has brothers who are circumcised, he will usually be circumcised too – most parents seem to want a matching set of penises in the family, though again there is no evidence that differences cause any psychological harm.

The safest time for circumcision

A very important question, and one that is not often asked by parents, is, what is the safest time for a baby to have the operation of circumcision? The answer to this is, the later the better. One thing is quite certain: the neonatal period (the first four weeks of life) is when it is *least* safe. The newborn baby has immature immunity, which makes him less than fully capable of fighting an infection. Also, his clotting mechanisms are immature.

Most babies get jaundice in the first few days of life, and one of the reasons for this is immaturity of the liver. One of the functions of the liver is to process the excess bilirubin that causes jaundice and eliminate it from the body. Significantly, the liver also produces clotting factors. It certainly seems illogical to trust the clotting mechanism of a baby who has jaundice – his liver function is demonstrably immature.

The only advantage of circumcision in the newborn period is that, as the baby is so small, he can't fight back. In a breathtaking piece of self-deception, some people believe that babies can't feel pain for the first few weeks, so no anaesthetic is necessary. Actually there is solid evidence that even a 26-week gestation foetus (three months before delivery) feels and responds to painful stimuli. There was also a study done in the UK that showed that babies who had had a circumcision as a newborn were more upset when getting their immunisation jab than babies who did not have the memory of such a painful experience.

If a circumcision is to be done, most paediatric surgeons would prefer to do it at the age of a year in a paediatric hospital with a paediatric anaesthetist in attendance. With an anaesthetic the surgeon can take his time and do a nice neat job, rather than doing it in a rush because the baby is screaming. It is still safer to have an anaesthetic and a circumcision in those circumstances at a year than it is to have an unanaesthetised neonatal circumcision.

Consequences

It is general knowledge in the paediatric community that occasionally babies die as a direct result of circumcision: up to sixteen babies die each year in the UK.

Other complications also occur. In a random study of a thousand families in England it was found that 22 percent of the boys circumcised had developed some complication from the procedure, including haemorrhages severe enough to require a blood transfusion.

It must be said, however, that the operation would be a good deal safer if it was taken more seriously. Too frequently it is delegated to the junior member of an obstetric team. Luckily, the penis has a very good blood supply and heals very quickly, and it is difficult for an infection to gain a foothold. Also, the skin is very mobile, and if too much is removed it usually makes very little functional difference, so most irregularities in technique are of no consequence. However, it is obvious that this part of the body is of tremendous psychological importance, so if mistakes are made, the scars remain not just on the body but also in the mind.

16

Sudden infant death syndrome (cot death)

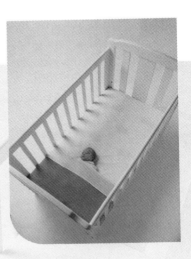

Nothing strikes fear into the hearts of parents more than the idea of cot death – sudden infant death syndrome (SIDS). Luckily, however, it is really quite rare. Fewer than one in 1000 babies are lost in this unexpected and insidious way. By definition, the babies die quietly, without a struggle, during sleep, and on careful examination of the circumstances and the baby, no cause can be found.

Statistics tell us that it is more common in boys than girls and during the cold months of the year. It is most common between the ages of two and four months, and the majority occur before six months. It is rare after one year.

Maternal factors can play a part – there is an increased risk if the mother smoked cigarettes during the pregnancy (the more cigarettes, the larger the risk), and a larger increase in risk if she was addicted to narcotics or barbiturates during the pregnancy.

You can paper the walls with theories as to the cause, but basically it probably comes down to failure of the breathing drive. Many factors feed into this final common pathway: some are genetic, some are not, and nobody has yet come near to satisfactorily explaining all cases. Nevertheless, these factors are worth noting, even at our present level of knowledge.

Put your baby on his back to sleep

Placing your baby on his side or him back in the cot seems without doubt to be more safe than placing him front down. There is no need to worry about the baby refluxing or vomiting and choking in these positions. Despite most babies being put on their backs to sleep nowadays, there are fewer deaths from choking and inhaling than before, not more. Babies have excellent reflexes to keep their airway clear – they will not inhale anything but air.

This is the single most important factor in reducing the incidence of SIDS. We are not sure why it works, but the theories include:

◇ it causes a reduced amount of obstruction to breathing
◇ expiratory air is not re-breathed in that posture
◇ it reduces heat stress
◇ there is an increase in blood flow to the brain
◇ it reduces the threshold for arousal (so babies don't sleep too deeply)
◇ it allows a more efficient action of the diaphragm.

Whatever the reason, it works, so put your baby 'Back to Sleep'.

Keep your baby's head uncovered while he's asleep

◇ Take any doonas, pillows, bumpers or soft toys that your baby could wriggle under out of the cot.

◇ Tuck your baby in with his arms out and the sheet under his armpits, so he can't slip under the covers. This reduces the possibility of coverings heat stressing or smothering him.

Don't smoke during or after pregnancy

◇ There is no doubt that smoking by either parent increases the risk of SIDS.

◇ If you do smoke, bed-sharing with your baby is an absolute no-no.

◇ Smoking also increases the likelihood of your baby getting serious illnesses so it's time you stopped if you haven't already. Call a support organisation like Quitline to help you succeed.

Don't overheat or overcool your baby

◇ Overheating (caused by a fever, too warm an environment or over-wrapping) seems to contribute to SIDS, so don't dress your baby in too many clothes. He should have on the same number of layers of clothing as you, not more.

◇ If your baby has a fever, reduce the number of layers.

◇ Remember that babies lose most heat through the head so be very wary of using bonnets, especially at night.

Breastfeeding may not protect (but it's still good)

The studies are confusing about whether or not breastfeeding is a protective factor, but do it anyway!

Breathing monitors

No one has proven that the electronic monitoring of babies makes any difference to the incidence of SIDS. Some babies fire off the alarm because they stop breathing, but no-one knows whether they would have died if left alone, or whether this 'apnoea' (Latin for 'no breathing') attack is even part of the same syndrome. Also, babies still die of cot death while being monitored – by the time the monitor alarm goes off, many of them cannot be revived.

We all share the same fear – paediatrician and printer, bus driver and journalist. Every parent, when the baby first sleeps through the night, will remember the hollow feeling in their stomach as they walk towards the baby's room to check that the baby is still breathing.

As already mentioned, it is not worthwhile electronically monitoring babies who have no special risks. There are usually too many terrifying false alarms, and the monitor is no guarantee of preventing SIDS. For very anxious parents a monitor may decrease the anxiety and for those it is an option to discuss with the paediatrician. I have seen some parents who would otherwise have watched the baby in shifts and never slept together again until the baby was two, but such anxiety is rare.

Put your baby 'Back to Sleep'

It is likely that in the future we will discover that there is an inborn or intrauterine factor that increases the likelihood for some infants to stop breathing in this way, and that the external factors just trigger the event. Research is now underway in many centres to find such an inborn error and so develop a screening test. Until that day comes, remember, the danger of SIDS is minuscule in comparison with the risks we run in our daily lives.

17

The secret fears all parents share

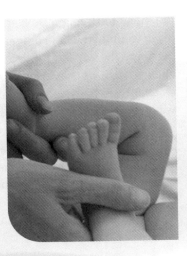

To a greater or lesser extent, being delivered of a baby with a congenital malformation or, even worse, suffering the loss of a baby, sets in train the grieving process. Its function is to help us adjust and recover and go back to living our lives in fullness and contentment.

The first response to this kind of tragedy is often total disbelief. Our mind plays tricks on us, telling us that it is not true and that we will soon wake up and all will be well.

Alas, soon this numbness wears off, to be replaced by anger and sadness. We feel cheated that this could happen to our baby. We examine the pregnancy in minute detail to try to find a reason, and even though there often is none, the feeling of responsibility and guilt remains.

Congenital malformations

About four in 100 babies are born with a congenital malformation. Of these, about half are serious and may threaten the life of the baby. It is a profoundly disappointing event and one that all prospective parents secretly fear. If the baby is seriously ill they also have to contend with the possibility that the baby may not survive. It is most important that the parents seek and get as much information about their baby's problem as they can, as soon as possible. The nights will be long enough without needless fears caused by not knowing what is going on, or not knowing what his prospects are, or what surgery is necessary and when it should be done. There are special advice and support groups for many of the more common malformations, such as cleft palate, Down's syndrome, or spina bifida; these groups can provide a lot of information as well as empathy and support.

Once the facts have been assimilated, the task of adjustment can begin. The parents need to see beyond the baby's problem to the little person himself. A single malformation often throws the whole baby out of focus – for a few days the parents can only see the cleft palate. The process of grieving often slows down the acceptance of the baby and makes the task of planning the future even harder.

Inevitably, the baby as a special and unique personality will emerge. The bonds form as strongly as ever, and the incredible resilience of human nature reveals and reasserts itself.

Losing a baby

Words cannot describe the pain of the loss of a baby. A stillbirth is just as traumatic – it is the loss of a baby you have never met face to face, but whom you know intimately.

After the baby has gone, there are few memories to help validate his life and make it seem more real, so the following steps are important. Try, if possible, to get photographs of the baby, to hold his image for the future. Try to get some physical contact with your baby, even after death. Within every bereaved parent there is a 'cuddle that must come out', and it is important to hold him and say goodbye, even if, at the time, this just seems to make it hurt more. Lastly, arrange a funeral, as you would for any other member of the family. This, too, underlines that the baby was a real person, loved and accepted by the family.

Remember, also, your poor friends. Some of them have no idea how to talk to you about your tragedy. They want to comfort you but they don't know how to start. They don't know whether to mention the baby or avoid the subject altogether.

They may delay phoning you while they try to figure it out. Suddenly weeks have passed and they are ashamed it's been so long and it becomes even more difficult for them to call. It's hard, but you may have to call them. Tell them about the baby and say that it's all right for them to talk to you about him – and not to mind if you cry when they do. They will be glad you have made it easier for them and they in turn will make it easier for you with their love and support. Other people, with the best will in the world, will say the wrong thing – but they are doing their best, so try to ignore their clumsiness.

No-one emerges from this experience unchanged. For some, marital relationships end, broken by the stress; for others the marriage becomes even stronger. But for everyone, life is changed. Many parents will say that the baby they lost has taught them more about life than those babies who remained. The poignancy of death taught them about passion, thoughtfulness and respect for life.

As we regard birth with a mixture of wonder and awe, joy and gratitude, so we see death is the other side of the same coin, equally full of wonder and awe, but mixed with loss, fear and finality.

It is the juxtaposition of these two staggering events that makes the loss of a newborn so difficult to assimilate.

Adjusting to the loss of a baby takes from several months to years, and, unfortunately, it gets worse before it gets better. Most parents feel that they are coping far less well after a few weeks than they did immediately following the birth, as their body and mind gradually stop protecting them from the full force of the loss. They may exhibit weird thoughts and behaviour, such as the desire to search for the baby or the need to protect the baby's grave from the weather. All these feelings are part of recovery.

It is a mistake to take medications (including tranquillisers) to blunt the pain. When the drugs are stopped the pain returns, and while it remains denied it will affect other parts of life and other relationships.

Eventually it has to be faced. When it is, the parents experience intense mood swings. The so-called pangs of grief will plunge them into misery and sadness. These pangs usually continue to be painful, but as the months go by they will occur less often. Though nothing can decrease the pain of loss, the best help is talking to each other or to someone who cares and understands. Loving relationships can be made or broken in such crises. As time passes, the parents usually find that they suffer pangs at different times – and the depressed one doesn't wish to disturb the coping one with his or her sadness. Communication slows down and the couple can drift apart.

Do not protect your partner from your feelings. You are in this together. As time goes on, you will realise that the human mind has healing capacities far beyond anything you can imagine. The deep physical pain of your loss diminishes and the memory of your baby becomes a precious part of your past, remembered with love but without hurt – a soft ache which is the sad price some have to pay to try and achieve the joys of parenthood.

Then perhaps it is time to think of another pregnancy.

> Many parents say that the baby they lost taught them more about life than the babies who lived

18

Postnatal depression

You've seen the advertisements. A beautiful woman, looking as if her day job is modelling for shampoo commercials, gently smiles down at her baby. The chubby baby smiles back with just the cutest little hint of drool emerging from her gummy grin. Their eyes are locked in love and bliss. This, truly, is what motherhood is all about.

I've got news for you. One of the best-kept secrets in maternity is that for 20 percent of mothers (one in five) things are very different. She is deeply miserable, desperately tired, anxious and frightened, and the baby does nothing but scream abuse at her. Somehow her life seems to be coming apart at the seams.

Very often she tells nobody, and nobody has a clue. Her parents and friends assume that because she has a healthy baby, she must be perfectly happy, and she is too ashamed to disillusion them. Her girlfriend rings her and the new mother tells her how happy she is and how well everything is going. They share a joke and she hangs up. Looking in the mirror, she realises it's three o'clock in the afternoon, she hasn't had a shower yet and is still in her nightdress. She looks around her. The house is a mess, with dust, dirty laundry and unwashed dishes everywhere. She feels and looks 20 years older than she did a few weeks ago. Her partner called an hour ago – he has to work late for the fourth time this week and he won't be home until eleven and don't worry about dinner. Then the baby starts to cry again.

Before the baby, everything was fine. She had a great relationship with her man, they were in love. She had a job that gave her satisfaction and a role in the world, and was capable and confident. Finances were tight but they never let it get them down. Then the baby arrived, and everything started to go wrong …

Postnatal depression is a catch-all phrase. Though it generally does not include the normal baby blues (which the majority of women get to some extent), it takes in the more severe depressive mood changes which last much longer, and which enter and interfere with every aspect of normal functioning. It does not include postnatal psychosis.

> Depression is a disorder of mood that may also affect thinking and bodily functions

Postnatal psychosis

This is a frightening and, luckily, rare disease in which the mother's sanity becomes unstable and she loses touch with reality. It is separate from and unrelated to postnatal depression. Depression is a disorder of mood that may also affect thinking and bodily functions; psychosis is a disorder of the thinking process itself. With postnatal psychosis there is usually a past or family history of mental illness, but the patient often does not realise that there is a problem.

In the throes of the disorder she may well be very depressed, paranoid or anxious. On the other hand, she may be wildly happy, active and feel euphoric. The hallmark of the disease is interference with normal thinking patterns – she will have delusions, hallucinations and other thoughts out of touch with reality. These thoughts can make her do strange things and possibly be a danger to herself and her baby. She requires hospitalisation and medication but will usually do well, recovering gradually over the course of months.

This disease can strike suddenly and unexpectedly and is completely unpredictable. It is also very rare.

Remember, even intense depression does not lead to psychosis. They are two separate diseases.

Postnatal depression

Within this hidden disease of motherhood there is a spectrum of severity, from the mild and transient 'fourth-day blues', to the severest form that can be crippling to a woman's whole life and wellbeing.

It reveals itself in a range of feelings, any combination of which may occur.

Deep depression and misery

This is just what it says.

Anxiety

A previously confident young woman can become anxious about everything – traffic, strangers, illness in the baby or herself … even household implements may seem threatening. This anxiety may be so prominent that it emerges before (or overshadows) the depression, and so completely incapacitating that the woman remains cowering and housebound and jumps at the ringing phone.

She may get panic attacks in public places, causing her to overbreathe (hyperventilate). The hyperventilation then causes physical symptoms of its own. She may be unable to sleep or her sleep is beset with nightmares. She may be terrified of harming herself or her baby and convinced she is going quite crazy.

Anger

It is not unreasonable for a mother locked into this cycle of depression and anxiety to turn her anger onto the person who has caused it all – the baby. Not surprisingly, this brings out strong guilt feelings and worsens the situation. There is often a lot of anger directed at the partner, too. After all, his life is relatively unchanged: he still goes out to work, still has his friends and leisure activities. Of course, now that there is another mouth to feed, he has very good reasons to do lots of overtime … quite apart from the fact that his partner is behaving strangely and aggressively towards him.

> Even intense depression does not lead to psychosis; they are two separate diseases.

Last and not least, she is angry at herself, and this destroys her self-esteem.

Loss of self-esteem

Our confident young woman, who is able to hold down a demanding and responsible job, has now been brought to her knees by a mere baby. What could be more destructive to her self-esteem? Some mothers don't even know they have postnatal depression. They just feel that their lives are a mess, and that they are responsible for it all.

Chronic fatigue

Nobody knows true fatigue like the new mother. Indeed, the hormones released by pregnancy and breastfeeding seem to interfere with the normal sleep/dream/wake patterns of the normal person.

Nobody can think straight when they're chronically fatigued – lack of sleep usually plays a big part in generating and maintaining postnatal depression. Exhaustion also makes it very hard to get anything done; housework is abandoned, meals are forgotten, and life just becomes too hard.

Causes and reasons

We can list all the factors that increase the possibility of postnatal depression, but none of these external factors can be called the cause. For most mothers, it is a mixture of intrinsic (within her) and extrinsic (external) factors that causes their depressive state.

Intrinsic factors

First and foremost, whether or not you will get the severer kind of depression depends on whether or not you have an inherent tendency towards it. In other words, how bad is your luck?

Some women seem to have an almost purely intrinsic type of depression. Everything seems to be going well, and there seems to be nothing in their circumstances that might provoke depression. Then a few days after the birth the depression sweeps over them, enveloping them like a dark blanket. Depression may even arrive during sleep. After their first pregnancy, many of these women learn to recognise the early signs – nothing seems to change unless they take medication. External factors seem to play only a small role in this kind of depression.

Extrinsic factors

Most depressed mothers have an intrinsic tendency to depression but also need at least some of these external factors to start the process:

⬦ Was the pregnancy or labour worse than expected?
⬦ Was the baby up to expectations?
⬦ Was the baby the wrong sex?
⬦ Is she a fractious screamer?
⬦ Is breastfeeding working?
⬦ What's in the mother's past history? Depression?
⬦ Is she an anxious type?
⬦ Were there fertility or obstetric worries?
⬦ How does she get on with her mother? Her partner?
⬦ How good were her self-esteem and coping skills before the pregnancy?
⬦ How secure are the family finances?

And on and on. None of these factors is particularly important in itself, but each one can play a part in bringing down a mother once the vicious depressive cycle begins.

If a woman has no intrinsic tendency to depression, many of the common external factors may come together and she will still feel no more than 'the baby blues'.

What to do

One of the problems with depression is that it also depresses the will to deal with it. You have to break the cycle.

Admit the problem

Accept that you have a problem that cannot and should not be ignored; it is a disease state that needs treatment. If you had pneumonia you would accept that you needed medical care, treatment, help and support with the baby. This disease is just the same. You owe it to your baby, your family and yourself to treat it seriously and allow your helpers to treat it properly.

Talk about it

It's very sad, but one of the symptoms of depression is an inability to get things done. This interferes with the most important part of the treatment, which is seeing someone about it. It is most important to sit and talk to someone who knows the issues involved. There is no doubt that the earlier you seek treatment, the sooner you can get back to being contented and feeling better about yourself.

> If a woman has no intrinsic tendency to depression, many of the common external factors may come together and she will still feel no more than 'the baby blues'.

Happily, nowadays, postnatal depression is being seen as the common disorder that it is, and more and more early childhood centre sisters, general practitioners, obstetricians and paediatricians quickly recognise the importance of the problem and know where to refer the sufferer.

⬥ For milder cases, the family doctor and self-help groups are usually enough.
⬥ For more severe cases, a visit to a psychiatrist can make all the difference. Unfortunately, many women feel that this stigmatises them as crazy, but this belief has no foundation. Not seeing a psychiatrist because of this feeling could mean cutting off a vital channel of help.

Get counselling

Remember, this disorder might be telling you something. It often brings to a head issues in your life that need resolution: now is the time to address the problems in your relationships with your mother, partner or baby. It is a time to look at what you expect from your family and your life. Try to make this time of unhappiness work for you so that you can improve the quality of your life when you emerge on the other side.

Get some help with the baby. Perhaps your partner can take some time off work to give you a hand – this will also help him understand how tough it is looking after a baby. Perhaps you have an extended family you can call upon to lend a hand. If there is no one, spending a little time in a mothercraft hospital might ease the load for a while.

Join a self-help group

For this problem, sharing your experiences and difficulties with others in a similar situation can be very helpful and reassuring. There are postnatal depression groups in most population centres – your early childhood centre nurse or family doctor will know how you can contact them.

Take antidepressant medicines (if your doctor recommends it)

Remember that feelings of depression and anxiety are generated by our brains, and that these feelings can be a response to internal chemical imbalances as well as to external events.

Depression is as much a disease as pneumonia. In both, an abnormal process is triggered off in the body, and various medications can help the body overcome its disease. Antidepressant drugs restabilise the chemical balance within the brain and this elevates the mood.

Antidepressants and breastfeeding

Most modern antidepressant drugs, monoamine oxidase inhibitors and anti-anxiety drugs are not excreted in any appreciable quantity in breastmilk, but check with your doctor anyway.

Consider stress management

Postnatal depression is also a disease of stress, so stress management tools can be used to control it.

◇ Practise time management. When you are confronted with a major task, such as housework, break it into small, bite-sized pieces and give yourself a reasonable, realistic timetable to get the work done. Do not overextend yourself, or have too high expectations of your ability to function.

◇ Learn to relax in a formalised way. Buy a relaxation tape, learn meditation or use breath control methods to try to get control of your anxiety.

◇ Take time out from the baby. Feed her, change her, put her in her cot and then go for a walk in the garden or listen to some music. No baby has come to harm because her mother takes ten minutes out for a quiet cup of coffee.

In conclusion

Here is a little gratuitous psychobabble that can be helpful because it happens to be true.

The brain's function is to think and generate feelings, and it does so as a response to the chemicals within itself. We are at the mercy of these substances in our day-to-day lives. Think about it. On a day when we feel unhappy, we look for a reason for the feeling, a 'hook' upon which to hang the emotion. On another day, under exactly the same conditions, we may feel contented, and we then choose to ignore the same hook, which is still there.

Of course events can and do change our mood. The point is that we do not necessarily have to accept the emotion we feel, and all the thoughts that go with it as valid and important. We can instead just watch it as dispassionately as possible and accept it for what it is, a chemical imbalance, a ripple on the surface of our life.

Easier said than done, especially when the emotion is a very powerful and intense one, such as depression. Nevertheless, stepping back from our feelings for a moment and replacing the thought 'I feel just terrible about my life' with the more accurate 'I feel depressed and a little anxious at the moment' is a useful process. It is a way to identify the raw individual emotions and remove the justifying thoughts that surround and support them. This reduces their power over us.

Also, realising that one is just depressed, not depressed *about* something, can be comforting. Similarly, recognising that our anxiety is free-floating rather than attached to a particular object or condition in our life can be a step towards controlling the hold this emotion has over us.

The later months: how babies and their needs develop

Watching our baby's development unfold is one of the most satisfying aspects of being a parent. Your little baby changes day by day, almost imperceptibly. Take lots of videos if you can. You'll miss your little baby when she's grown …

At birth

At birth your baby lies on her front with both her knees tucked under her abdomen and her head to the side. She tries, but cannot lift her head off the mattress. If you turn her over and pull her up by her hands (it's quite safe), her head falls backwards.

She has active 'primitive' reflexes:

◇ If you tickle the palm of her hand, it will clench in the grasp reflex.

◇ If her head is allowed to flop backwards, she will demonstrate a well-developed startle (Moro) reflex – she throws her arms out, arches her back and then brings her hands together.

◇ If she is held up to stand, she will make clumsy walking movements with her feet (this is sometimes hard to elicit).

◇ She can't yet turn to sound, but will gaze fixedly towards the light.

At four weeks

◇ She is still trying to raise her head from the mattress, and when she is pulled to sit, she has a little head control.

◇ Her grasp reflex is still present, but her other primitive reflexes are starting to disappear.

◇ She will now follow your face through a narrow arc, and in the next week or so, she will start to smile back at you if you smile at her first.

At eight weeks

◇ She can lift her head off the mattress when she is on her front, and her head control is much improved.

◇ She has now lost her grasp and walking reflexes and only part of her startle reflex remains.

◇ She can clasp her hands in the midline and can put them in her mouth.

◇ Her eyes fix and focus and she can follow you with her eyes through a wider arc.

◇ She is starting to chuckle and coo.

At three months

By this time your baby is definitely a person, and your relationship with her is solid. She knows you and you know her. Being the mother of a newborn baby is hard work, but from here on the workload eases and the fun really begins.

Your baby's awareness, understanding and ability to communicate with things around her are increasing day by day. Her joy and enjoyment of things around her, especially her mother, are also increasing. It has been known for many years that mothers and babies develop increasing 'synchronicity' in the early months – that is, they're more in tune with each other.

Observe a typical scene at home. The baby is propped up by cushions on the sofa, safe and comfortable. She looks up and finds her mother busy in the kitchen (or on her laptop). She gazes at her intensely. After a few moments she makes cooing noises and waves her arms briefly. Her mother looks up and looks directly at her. She raises her eyebrows, increases her vocalisation to her and waves both arms in a circular manner. She draws her mother to her and she moves towards her, speaking in a high welcoming voice. A sunshine grin wreathes her face, her arms are swinging rhythmically and are joined by her legs stretched in extension, toes curling. Mother comes closer and her hands hold her thighs as she gazes deep into her eyes, smiling to her smile, cooing to her coos. She talks to her, her voice rising varying in tone and pitch – her voice does the same, following her. Her limbs settle down into a relaxed pose and her movements on her thighs slow and stop. She looks away briefly and plays with her hands, then glances quickly back to her and starts again, grinning and talking. She responds. This goes on rhythmically for a few more moments, then she glances away, looks out of the window and ignores her. She kisses her briefly and goes back to her task.

> Close interaction between mother and baby is well developed by 3–4 months

A few minutes later she glances at her, makes cooing noises and starts waving her arms and the 'dance' starts again. This close interaction of mother and baby can be observed from the early months, but by three to four months it is well developed. The baby is practising social skills and learning as much as she can from her mother's face and voice. She is still not very good at taking all the intense interactions she has to offer her, so she regularly 'switches off' – mothers almost unconsciously fit in with this pattern and withdraw. Studies have shown that this cyclical behaviour, the rising and falling of interaction, occurs regularly and relatively predictably.

Babies behave completely differently with inanimate objects: the smooth rising and falling rhythms of interaction are not there. They pay intense attention to new, interesting objects, interspersed with abrupt, brief periods of inattention where they will turn away. Then suddenly their attention will return and they will make jerky abrupt movements and swipe at the object. Then they will turn away again. Because they get no feedback from the object, their relationship with it is totally different from their relationship with people.

Now is a good time to give babies little mobiles and objects on strings above them in their pram. Their arm movements are pretty inaccurate at this age, but from three to four months they will start to try and grasp objects that they can see – the more brightly coloured and interesting the better. At this age the grasp reflex has gone; it has been replaced by a true voluntary holding movement. If you put a rattle in your baby's hand it will stay there for a short while at three months and for much longer by four months.

One of the most interesting objects to babies at this age is their own hands. 'Hand regard' (a developmental milestone) starts early, and is well developed by four months. This is helped by the increasing strength of muscles in the neck; they can now hold the baby's head straight when she is lying on her back, rather than letting it fall to one side or the other.

Her head control is better in all planes. If you pull her up by her hands from lying on her back she will hold her head completely in the line of her body at three to four months, and when she is sitting up her head is straight and she looks around. Her back is also starting to straighten; there is only a little curvature in the lower lumbar area now.

If you place your baby face downwards she will raise her head and look straight ahead. Her chest is off the surface and her weight is on her forearms, legs stretched out behind her. By sixteen weeks she can start doing the 'flying baby' trick, where she arches her back so much that both arms and both legs are off the ground and she is resting entirely on her abdomen.

She really is pretty smart, but she can be a little too smart for her own good. At this age many babies take their first tumble as they learn to roll over on the change table precisely when their mother is the other side of the room. Luckily, most babies bounce and come to no harm. But it's best to never leave her alone on beds, the change table or in the bath without a hand on her. At this age babies are learning motor skills rapidly, and neither you nor they know their capabilities from day to day. Be especially careful when she is in the bath – vigorous leg movements can submerge her rapidly if her position is unstable.

Now she doesn't miss a thing: she catches sight of people as soon as they enter the room and her eyes follow them as they move out of sight, waiting expectantly for them to return. When she sees her feeds being prepared or the breast being uncovered at feed time she gets visibly excited and expectant.

Indeed, her understanding is now enough for her to have expectations about familiar circumstances, and she will feel thwarted and upset if her expectations are not met. If you take her into a new room she will gaze around with interest and a little shyness or uncertainty. Showing babies of this age nose-cleaning cotton buds was used as part of a developmental assessment at one time – the baby is meant to squirm and turn her head away.

'Hand regard' starts early and is well developed by 4 months

Her eyes will follow a dangling object now through a full 180 degrees, but up to four months she is not very good at spotting small objects.

At long last the evening periods of distress and unsettled behaviour are diminishing, if not disappearing. The evening is now a time for enjoyable play. The baby has learned to cope with more stimulation and interaction from people and things around her, and the people around her are more sensitive to her abilities to cope, and they pace their interactions, unconsciously, so as not to overload her.

She's actually so interested in things around her that feeding can start to become difficult – she turns to every noise and goes on and off the breast at the slightest provocation. This period requires patience, and the knowledge that this inattention will diminish over the next few weeks as she gets more used to the world around her. Feeding can also be less 'on demand' – her feedings can be gently manoeuvred (to some degree) into a more reasonable schedule.

Many babies are now sleeping for longer periods; many will have an eight-hour sleep at night. But the range of normal still remains very wide, and if your baby is still waking you twice, you should probably accept this at least for a little longer. Many babies will appear to be prolonging their periods between feeds and sleeping through and then hit a 'growth spurt' where frequent feeds start again. Growth spurt is the wrong name: what is more likely is that the baby requires more breastmilk. The way to increase breastmilk supply is by completely emptying the breast and increasing sucking stimulation to the nipple. The more the breast is emptied completely, the more milk will be produced next time, so these brief periods of increased sucking will lift the milk supply to a slightly higher level to meet the baby's needs for the first weeks of life. The level then gradually plateaus as the breast and baby work together to achieve a satisfactory growth rate.

At this age it is not yet necessary for the baby to have solids – gram for gram there is more growth in a stomach full of milk than there is in a stomach full of solids. In the past, some people believed that feeding the baby solids in the evening would help her sleep through the night. Well-conducted studies have shown that this makes no difference whatever.

It is possible at this age to start gently manipulating your baby into sleeping for longer periods. Do not respond to her every groan, burp and whimper. It is a good idea to get her to sleep longer (if you can!) before five to six months of age, when she learns manipulative behaviour and can start playing night games with you, but at three months, when she is still driven by instinct, it may be a little too early. It is certainly worth a try, though.

At six months

The six-month-old baby is an absolute charmer. Follow-up consultations with her in my office are a real pleasure. She comes into the consulting room in her mother's arms with a big, gummy grin and sits on her knee opposite me. She views her doctor with an amused, piercing gaze and watches intently as I talk to her mother. After a few moments she coughs gently and then, if she doesn't get any attention, starts slapping the top of the desk with her little hand. Naturally everyone looks at her and her grin gets even bigger, puffed with self-importance. As long as she is on her mother's knee she is fearless and extroverted, dominating the room with her presence.

Grasping

Her hands are getting more useful to her. Her grasp is simple at six months – all her fingers work together in a raking movement to pick up an object. In a month or so her forefinger and thumb will start to be used separately and she will develop a useful pincer grip. At that time she will also start to pass things from hand to hand. However, when offered a second object she will drop whatever is in her hand and take the new one. She won't use her

opposite hand to help her hold on to both things at once for another month or two.

Safety

Everything she picks up will now go into her mouth, not necessarily because she is teething but because her mouth is one of the main sensory organs she uses to explore her world. Soon she will start exploring with her fingers too, and with this behaviour comes new dangers. She will swipe and grasp at anything within her reach; so if you are sitting at the table with her – beware the hot coffee cup! Move it. Remember, she will soon be crawling or rolling across the floor and electrical outlets or loose tablecloths hanging from tables can all be poked or pulled. Now is the time to start thinking of safety – a playpen might be useful.

Sleep

As her comprehension increases, she spends more and more of her waking time exploring her world. Her naps during the day will start to shorten and she might become harder to put down at night once she knows that she gets to stay up for longer by fussing. An unchanging ritual that will short-circuit these evening games is a good idea.

Separation anxiety may start for some babies at this age – a bedtime friend, such as a teddy, may offer her the night-time company she craves. And leave her bedroom door open, so that she can hear the household nearby. If she is to have a babysitter she should meet her (or him) before she goes to bed, so that if she wakes in the night she is familiar with the person who comes to comfort her.

Once asleep, most babies will sleep reasonably soundly at this age. If she is still waking for night breastfeeds it's likely that she's doing it more for the company than because she's hungry. If you desperately need sleep you might try putting a stop to it by sending Dad in instead. If it doesn't work, don't push it yet. However, you might need the rest – at nine months night waking often restarts!

Food

With her new useful grasp she now starts to feed herself with a biscuit or even hold a spoon. With the introduction of solids she will start to explore not only tastes and textures but wonderful new experiences like the feel of pumpkin in her hair or how it (and you) look when the rest is thrown onto the floor. If the performance appears to be enjoyed, it will be repeated long after the audience has stopped appreciating it.

Solids are nutritionally useful to a baby at this age. Beyond five or six months, breastmilk does not contain enough iron for her. Iron-containing cereals are usually the first 'solid' food she will have, before she tries out more diverse tastes. She will be able to chew after six or seven months, so she can try true solids.

Babies soon remember various foods and develop likes or dislikes. Most babies can start drinking from a cup at this age too.

Remembering

The six-month-old baby's understanding of the world is developing and expanding. When she drops something on the floor, she will watch where it goes and will try to recover it. Even though it is out of sight she still remembers it is there. The same memory process lets her enjoy peek-a-boo games, and she will giggle in anticipation at an approaching tickling finger. She will start to smile at her image in a mirror, and after a few weeks will try to pat it. Her speech becomes more distinct and Dad will become convinced that 'da' is directed at him (but he is wrong – at least for a few more months).

Strength

Her back is now strong enough to support her when she is sitting up, but this is a complex milestone, and develops gradually – first comes the ability to straighten the back, and then, over a period of months, comes increasing stability.

Soon the baby can use her hands while sitting and also twist and turn without overbalancing. Life is much more interesting now she can hold her body upright. She can gaze around the room and play with her toys far more efficiently.

At first, she tends to lean forward on her hands, and if she tries to use them she is likely to topple over and not be able to get back up. When lying on her front, she is up on her hands – chest and abdomen off the floor.

By seven months she can bear her weight on one hand while using the other to reach for a toy. She can usually roll from her front to her back by now, but it will be a month or so longer before she does the reverse.

When held upright, she will bear her weight on her feet and start to bounce.

It is only a short time before she will learn to crawl.

At nine months

At nine months your baby is teetering on the brink of toddlerhood. At last she has discovered what her legs are for, and the day is not long enough to cram in all the necessary practice.

At the beginning, at eight to nine months, getting herself up is something of a struggle, but once helped up with hands placed against a piece of furniture, she will stand there beaming and laughing as she sees that her two-dimensional world has now got three. Unfortunately she needs help getting down too, but after a few bumps and rolls she learns to fold in the middle and drop onto her bottom.

A few weeks later she can pull herself up and, a little while after that, make sideways steps and start cruising round the furniture. If you haven't made your house a safe place already, do it now. Buy the stair gates, before you walk in from the kitchen and find your little mountaineer halfway up the stairs, doggedly climbing. Anything up high must be put out of reach of little hands: saucepan handles, kettles, heated towel rails, irons (beware that cord), rubbish bins, curtains and tablecloths are all handholds when you only have cruise control. Watch out also for house plants – be sure that the ones in reach can be eaten safely, leaves and all.

Most babies of this age can sit stably, and recover if they lean forward and (usually) if they lean sideways. Even so, *never* trust this ability in the bath – it only takes a moment to topple over, so always supervise. As time goes on they can move in and out of the sitting position with greater ease, going from the sitting position to prone and back again. Many babies also learn to 'commando crawl' at this age, creeping forward on their tummy.

Hands are now of more use, and as her manipulation skills increase, the mouthing of objects will tend to diminish. She develops a neat little finger/thumb grasp and can pick up small beads or even pieces of thread. Not only that, but at last she learns to release things as well. Soon the favourite game of tossing everything out of her cot and waiting hopefully for them to be put back in will start in earnest. Give her two cubes, one at a time – instead of throwing away the first in order to take the second, she will now take them both, look at and compare them, then bang them together.

Though she may well still be breastfeeding, she loves eating solids, especially if she is allowed to feed herself. So offer her a plate of food with her own spoon. True, the plate becomes a drum and much of the food ends up on the floor or in her hair (especially if it is not her favourite), but by this age she is capable of satisfying her appetite for both food and experiences at the same time. It's also time to learn to drink from a cup – the more practice she has, the more skilled she will become. As a compromise, a beaker with a spout will certainly keep the bib and floor drier.

Most babies at this age now need only four feeds a day. This is a common time to move towards weaning, but most will still breastfeed for at least the first and the last feed of the day (which is a good night settling technique).

Sleep patterns, which for many families had become a non-issue for the last few months, can sometimes become a problem again at this age. Night waking can restart as the baby learns that this results in solo playtime with mother. Usually parents put it down to 'teething' at the beginning, and soon the habit is established. Don't be fooled by teething. It is reasonable to accept a little discomfort in the gum for a few hours as the new tooth emerges, but night upon night of unsettled behaviour is much more likely to be behavioural in nature. A no-nonsense approach of loving but perfunctory attention should soon help the noisy one decide that it isn't worth the trouble. But definitely no rewarding feeds or bottles in the cot at this age.

> Anything up high must be completely out of reach

Her comprehension of the world continues to expand – it will extend to daily tasks such as getting dressed, when she can hold out her arm for a sleeve or her foot for a sock. Her memory is improving and she understands the meaning of a number of words. She knows the names of members of the family and understands simple commands, such as 'Sit down', or questions, such as 'Where is Daddy?'. She may object if you get the words of a nursery rhyme wrong. Her speech is now in double syllables, such as 'mama' and 'dada', and she uses them correctly more often. She can also tentatively imitate sounds made by mother. She can wave bye-bye with a smile and simple games like pat-a-cake and peek-a-boo are solid favourites.

Time spent reading picture books to her is now important. Some evidence suggests that depriving a baby of books and pictures at this age can have a lasting impact on her ability to learn. So the bedtime ritual of the storybook is not only a time for cuddles and conversation – it also lays the foundation for a lifetime of learning and love of knowledge.

At one year

When your baby turns one, it is cause for celebration! She has worked very hard being a baby, and for you, the year seems to have disappeared in the twinkling of an eye. Everyone remembers their baby's first birthday – the one little candle (and soon after, the toes of the little foot) sticking into a pink or blue birthday cake. The door of toddlerhood now stands wide open, and your baby is straining to walk through it.

Walking

Walking is a major milestone, and by a year most babies will be on their feet as often as possible. Usually, they will still need help from a friendly hand or some friendly furniture if they are to get very far. Some babies, however, learn that faster progress can be achieved using their bottoms and an arm, or hands and feet (like a bear), and will be wary of standing up. Very sensible too, judging by the bumps and bruises on the bodies of the early walkers.

Though many babies will be walking by about thirteen months, there is no need to be too concerned if your baby doesn't walk until several months after that. Like toilet training, if you just wait, it will come. A lot depends on the baby's confidence – she may be timid, or have some memory of being knocked down by a flying sibling during an early attempt – or her muscles may not be ready. The first steps will be ungainly, teetering and tottering on the edge of balance, often ending up with a bump on the bottom. By now, of course, sitting is solid as a rock. She can pivot and turn, leaning left and right, and it is unusual for her to fall over.

A word of warning: don't get too anxious about what babies 'should' be doing at any given age. What is average is not necessarily what is appropriate for your baby. Seek help only if your child appears to be slow in many fields of development, not just one or two.

More skilled

Your one-year-old's fine motor skills are improving day by day. She has now learned to hold two or three cubes in her hand and, if handed another, will attempt to hang on to them all. She will try to build a tower of two blocks – and sometimes she will succeed. She loves to take blocks and put them into and out of a container, hour after hour. She also likes to hand her mother objects just so that she will give them back; this can also be repeated over and over again. She likes to make marks on paper with a crayon but is not yet up to scribbling.

Speech

Most babies at this age understand many words but only speak two or three understandable ones. They have numerous words that are not understandable (to others), and will start making long, rambling speeches, complete with meaningful gestures, appropriate inflections and relevant facial movements. What a pity only they know what they are talking about!

Intelligence

It is at this age that clues emerge as to the baby's intellect. These clues, however, are not related to motor ability (that is, the timing of milestones such as sitting or walking). Many children with advanced motor skills have no special mental capacity, and most who are delayed by a few months are quite normal intellectually.

Don't get too anxious about what babies 'should' be doing at any given age. Seek help only if your child appears to be slow in many fields of development, not just one or two.

The clue to intelligence lies in the quality of the child's interaction with the world around her. The intelligent child concentrates well on a task and has a determination to succeed. She looks at the world with enthusiasm and intensity. She is confident and poised, and is thoughtful and inventive in seeking solutions to everyday problems.

Comprehension

Many babies really enjoy pointing gestures at this age – it usually gets a great reaction from the audience. Their comprehension now also allows them to run simple errands: 'Get your teddy'; answer questions: 'Where is Daddy?'; and obey a few commands: 'Give me a kiss!'

One-year-olds also know how to get your attention, and their life starts to revolve around that activity. They learn to turn on the television when you're in the next room, dump their food on the floor if you seem to be overly keen on them eating it, and they are generally very sensitive to subtle pressures and expectations.

'No!'

This is a time for rigid discipline – of yourself. Your little child is struggling into a new era of independence. She has learned the power of 'No!', and it may well become one of her favourite words. Your task is to accept and support the fact that your baby wishes to become an individual who can make her own decisions, and control her environment, but at the same time not let her negativism be rewarded so it becomes an end in itself.

Imagine the surge of power you feel when you first learn that you can actually manipulate your mother's behaviour! But also imagine the rush of fear when you realise you are independent. As the baby swings between the two emotions, her poor parents are caught in the middle.

This negativism is very obvious in the consulting room. At nine months you can examine a baby easily, and she will smile broadly at you in an open, outgoing way. At a year, she becomes shy and worried. If you look at her directly, she will shrink from you. If you attempt to examine her, she will howl and struggle. She needs to be approached gently and obliquely, and needs to be given time to accept that you will not harm her.

Changes

You may also notice her new negativity towards nappy changing. It's not that she doesn't want her nappy changed, it's just that avoiding it seems like a good idea at the time.

Similarly with feeding: as soon as your one-year-old perceives that it is most important to you that she eats well, she will eat almost nothing. She will do anything for a good reaction from her parents. Having said that, toddlers often have small appetites anyway. My advice is to offer her food at regular intervals; if she chooses not to eat it, it should be given to the cat. If you make a fuss or start using games or rewards to get her mouth open, you are on the slipperiest of slopes, and it is inevitable that you will end up in a heap at the bottom. Only by ignoring the problem will it go away. Do not worry about friendly advice regarding how much a child should eat. Healthy, active children eat what is necessary if it is offered; they don't starve or become nutrient-deficient. If you can't handle your toddler refusing food at times, the problem might be yours, not hers!

Epilogue: Zen and the art of parenting

With children, as with our own life, every age has both special joys and aspects we would prefer to forget. It is tempting to consider every stage our babies go through as merely preparation for the next phase of development.

Suddenly they look us in the eye and say goodbye – and we wonder where their childhood went. Their childhood went while we were waiting for them not to do this or that, to be a bit more mature, and not get in our way so much. It went when they screamed all night with earache, when they ran their tricycle into the furniture and when they refused to go to bed and stay there.

Our babies are our immortality, right here and now. They are also the best personal growth experience available. Anybody who wants to tread a spiritual pathway that will hold up a mirror to the person he or she truly is, need search no further than having a baby. There is no better teacher anywhere. We can be anyone we like to our friends – compassionate, patient, sensible – but our little ones will see through the façade and show us who we really are. Like no-one else, our babies can push our secret, psychic buttons.

Parenthood is an essential part of existence, for those who wish to grow and for those who would rather avoid it.

Don't miss the opportunity or the experience.

I wish you joy and enough sleep.

Acknowledgements

Over the years my knowledge and insight, such as it is, has been honed by the many parents and babies I have met. The sharp edges of theoretical knowledge absorbed from medical books and journals have been smoothed by daily contact with these more proficient teachers. Thanks also to the many parents who contributed vignettes of their experiences or allowed their babies to be photographed or sent in photos, especially Sylvia and Howard Amoils, Sharon and Scott Beynon, Jenny Balomatis and John Haitidis, Maria and Frank Failla, Hazel and Gary Gordon, Becky and Huw Jones, Senka Kajtez-Mathews and Mark Naglost, Steven and Terry Kruyer, Lesley and Patrick O'Connor, Michelle and Brendan Ring, Nikki and Mark Sullivan, Beatriz and Chris Vlattas, and Sharon and Jay Weber. And special thanks to Dawn Michel of Moving Images Photography, and to SIDS and Kids.

Thanks too to the colleagues who took the time to review the parts of the text in which they are expert, especially Professor John Zielger (immunologist), Professor James McKenna (anthropologist: bed-sharing section), Dr Debbie Kennedy (Mothersafe: drugs in breastmilk), Ms Joy Heads (lactation consultant: breastfeeding text), and Ms Judy Kotowski (breastfeeding pictures).

Thanks too to the staff at Finch Publishing, to Sarah Shrubb for editing, and special thanks to Diane Young, who sent me in the right direction.

Thanks and love to Tamara and my girls, Georgina and Isabella, who taught me how wonderful a happy, supportive family can be, even though I always seem to be too busy to hold up my end of the deal.

References

PART II What happens in the hospital

Apple, R.D., *Mothers and Medicine: A Social History of Infant Feeding 1890–1950*, University of Wisconsin Press, 1987

Cox, Sue, *Breastfeeding: I Can Do That*, Taslac, Tasmania, 1997

Leaflets from the Australian Breastfeeding Association (formerly the Nursing Mothers of Australia Association – NMAA), available at *www.breastfeeding.asn.au*

PART III Evolution and babies

Bartoshuk, L.M. and Beauchamp, G.K., 'Chemical Senses', *Annual Review of Psychology* (1994), 45:419–49

Hrdy, S.B., *Mother Nature: Natural Selection & The Female of the Species*, Chatto & Windus, 1999

Jelliffe, D.B. and Patrice Jelliffe, E.F., *Human Milk in the Modern World*, Oxford University Press, 1978

McKenna, J. and Gartner, L., 'Sleep Location and Suffocation: How Good Is The Evidence?', *Pediatrics* (2000), vol. 105, 4:917–19 (there is also excellent reading on Professor Mckenna's website: *www.nd.edu/~alfac/mckenna*)

McKenna, J.J., 'Cultural influences on infant and childhood sleep biology and the science that studies it: Toward a More Inclusive Paradigm', in Laughlin, J., Marcos, C. and Carroll, J. (eds), *Sleep and Breathing In Children and Pediatrics*, Marcel-Dekker Publications, 2000

Shlain, L., *The Alphabet versus the Goddess: The Conflict between the Word and Image*, Penguin, 1998

Watson, Lyall, *Jacobson's Organ*, Penguin, 2000

Winberg J. and Porter, R.H., 'Olfaction and human neonatal behaviour: clinical implications', *Acta Paediatrica* (1998), 87:6–10

Part IV What happens at home

Heine, R.G., Jaquiery, A., Lubitz. L., Cameron, D.J.S. and Catto-Smith, A.G., 'Role of Gastro-oesophageal reflux in infant irritability,' Archives of Diseases of Childhood (1995), 73:121–25

Lucassen, P.L.B., Assendelft, W.J.J., Gubbels, J.W., van Eijk, J.T.M., van Geldrop, W.J. and Knuistingh Neven, A., 'Effectiveness of Treatments for Infantile Colic: systematic review', British Medical Journal (1998), 316:1563–69

McKenzie S., 'Troublesome crying in infants: effect of advice to reduce stimulation', British Medical Journal (1991), 66:1416–20

National Health & Medical Research Council, Immunisation: Myths and Realities, Commonwealth Publications Office, 1999

Poland, R.L., 'The question of routine circumcision', New England Journal of Medicine (1990), 322:1312–15

Schoen, E.J., 'The status of circumcision of newborns', New England Journal of Medicine (1990), 322:1308–12

Contacts

Australia

Australian Breastfeeding Association – Lactation Resource Centre
03 9885 0855
lrc@breastfeeding.asn.au
www.breastfeeding.asn.au

Drug information. For specialised independent advice and information on drugs in relation to lactation or for children, contact the Drug Information Service in your state. These are based at a Women's or Children's Hospital, whose telephone numbers are:

ACT   02 6244 3333
NSW 02 9845 2701 Children's Hospital, Westmead
       02 9382 6717 Royal Hospital for Women
NT   08 8922 8424
QLD 07 3840 8226 Mater Hospital
       07 3253 7098 Royal Brisbane Hospital
       07 3253 7300 Royal Women's Hospital
SA   08 8204 7222
TAS 03 6222 8737
VIC 03 9550 2361 Monash Medical Centre
       03 9345 5208 Royal Children's Hospital
       03 9344 2277 Royal Women's Hospital
WA   08 9340 2743

For information on recreational drugs or drugs of addiction, contact the Alcohol and Drugs Information Service in your state.

Early Childhood Health Clinics. These are listed under 'Early Childhood Health Centres' in your local telephone directory.

Hospital websites. The website of your state children's hospital is a good resource:
Mater Children's Hospital, Brisbane
    http://www.mater.org.au/our_mater_hospitals/mch.html
Princess Margaret Hospital for Children, Perth *www.pmh.wa.gov.au*

Royal Hospital for Children, Melbourne *www.rch.unimelb.edu.au*
Sydney Children's Hospital *www.sch.edu.au*
The Children's Hospital, Westmead *www.chw.edu.au*
Women and Children's Hospital, Adelaide *www.wch.sa.gov.au*

Mothercraft Centres and their help lines:
Tresillian Family Care Centre 1800 637 357; *www.tresillian.net*
Karitane 1800 677 961
Canterbury Parents Help Line 02 9787 5255

Poisons Information Service in all states is available on 13 11 26.

SIDS (Sudden Infant Death Research Foundation) 1300 308 307.

New Zealand

Plunketline (a 24-hour parents' advice line) 0800 933 922

Hospital websites
Canterbury Health *http://www.chl.govt.nz/*
Christchurch Women's Hospital *http://www.chl.govt.nz/cwh/*
Listing of Public Hospitals: New Zealand Hospitals Online
  http://www.nzhealth.co.nz/publichospitals/index.html
National Women's Hospital, Auckland *http://www.nwhealthinfo.co.nz/*
New Zealand Paediatric Hospital: Starship Children's
  Hospital *http://www.starship.org.nz/*

Breastfeeding *www.lalecheleague.org.LLLNZ/*

Maternity Services Consumer Council *www.maternity.org.nz*

New Mothers' Support Groups *www.newmother.org.nz*

NZ Medicines Safety Authority *www.medsafe.govt.nz*

For a more extensive list of links, go to *www.homebirth.org.nz/links/htm*

Other Finch titles of interest

Parenting

Adolescence

A guide for parents

Michael Carr-Gregg and Erin Shale

In this informative and wide-ranging book, the authors help parents understand what is happening for young people and how to deal with it. ISBN 1876451 351

A Handbook for Happy Families

A practical and fun-filled guide to managing children's behaviour

Dr John Irvine

In this wise and humorous approach to parenting, the author tackles the commonest problems with children of all ages. He also presents his innovative and well-tested 'Happy/sad face discipline system', which draws families together rather than dividing them. ISBN 1 876451 416

Raising Boys

Why boys are different – and how to help them become happy and well-balanced men

In his international bestseller, Steve Biddulph examines the crucial ways that boys differ from girls. He looks at boys' development from birth to manhood and discusses the warm, strong parenting and guidance boys need. ISBN 0646314 181

Raising Boys Audio

A double-cassette set read by Steve Biddulph.

ISBN 1 876451 254

Fathering from the Fast Lane

Practical ideas for busy dads

Dr Bruce Robinson

The pressures of working life today mean that many fathers are not spending the time with their children that they would like. This book presents practical and straightforward ways to improve this situation. In this collection of valuable fathering ideas, over 75 men from various backgrounds speak about how they balance demanding jobs with being a good dad. ISBN 1876451 211

Parenting after Separation

Making the most of family changes

Jill Burrett

So much parenting now takes place from two households, following separation. This book offers positive approaches to helping children and making the most of these family changes.

ISBN 1876451 378

Father and Child Reunion

How to bring the dads we need to the children we love

Dr Warren Farrell

This book calls for a rejoining of families (and of children with parents who can care for them) by creating equal opportunities for men as parents. ISBN 1876451 327

Bullybusting

How to help children deal with teasing and bullying

Evelyn Field reveals the 'six secrets of bully-busting', which contain important life skills for any young person. Activities introduce young readers to new skills in communicating feelings, responding to stressful situations and building a support network. An empowering book for parents and their children (5-16 years). ISBN 1876451 041

On Their Own

Boys growing up underfathered

Rex McCann

For a young man, growing up without an involved father in his life can leave a powerful sense of loss. *On Their Own* considers the needs of young men as they mature, the passage from boyhood to manhood, and the roles of fathers and mothers.

ISBN 1876451 084

Fathers After Divorce

Building a new life and becoming a successful separated father

Michael Green

'Comprehensive, beautifully clear, fair and friendly ... a separated man's best friend.' *Steve Biddulph*

ISBN 1876451 009

Beginning Fatherhood

A guide for expectant fathers

Warwick Pudney and Judy Cottrell

For a man about to start the most important job of his life, this book is a commonsense guide to understanding the stages of pregnancy, what the mother-to-be needs, and much more. ISBN 1876451 017

Chasing Ideas:

The fun of freeing your child's imagination

Christine Durham teaches thinking skills to children, and in this book she encourages parents and teachers to see how discussing ideas with their children (aged 4 to 14) can be an enjoyable and creative activity for everyone.

ISBN 1876451 181

Fear-free Children

Dr Janet Hall draws on real-life case studies to help parents overcome specific fears and anxieties that their children have, such as fear of the dark, fear of being alone or fear of animals. ISBN 1876451 238

Fight-free Families

Dr Janet Hall provides solutions to conflicts in a wide range of family ages and situations, from young children through to adolescents. ISBN 1876451 22X

The Happy Family

Ken and Elizabeth Mellor provide simple, easy-to-use ways to manage our families well, including: understanding and changing your family patterns; creating balance between family life and work; learning from your childhood experience of families; handling family conflicts; and working together as a parenting team. ISBN 1876451 122

Easy Parenting

Ken and Elizabeth Mellor offer many practical skills and approaches, including different ways of loving your child; using repetition to help children learn; developing your child's self-esteem; struggling with children for their benefit; managing conflicts between siblings; and effective ways to discipline. ISBN 1876451 114

ParentCraft

A practical guide to raising children well (Second edition)

Ken and Elizabeth Mellor's comprehensive guide to parenting provides clear information on issues such as communicating with children, a healthy (no-hitting) approach to discipline, the stages of child development and skills in managing families. ISBN 1876451 19X

Women's health

Your pregnancy

A week-by-week guide to a worry-free pregnancy
Alison Somers

This is an informative, week-by-week guide with whimsical illustrations. Its calendar format provides daily entries for planning and recording the important events of this special time. The perfect gift! ISBN 1876451 36X

Motherhood

Making it work for you
Jo Lamble and Sue Morris provide useful approaches for mothers to deal with difficulties in everyday family life

and to help make motherhood a rewarding, enjoyable experience. ISBN 1876451 033

Relationships

Women Can't Hear What Men Don't Say

Destroying myths, creating love

Dr Warren Farrell provides a remarkable communication program to assist couples in understanding and loving each other more fully. ISBN 1876451 319

Side by Side

How to think differently about your relationship

Jo Lamble and Sue Morris provide helpful strategies to overcome the pressures that lead to break-ups, as well as valuable advice on communication, problem-solving and understanding the stages in new and established relationships. A marvellous book for young people. ISBN 1876451 092

Children's health

Kids Food Health:

Nutrition and your child's development

The authors, Dr Patricia McVeagh – a paediatrician – and Eve Reed – a dietitian – present the parents of children from newborns to teenagers with the latest information on the impact of diet on health, growth, allergies, behaviour and physical development.

Kids Food Health 1: *The first year* ISBN 1876451 149

Kids Food Health 2: *From toddler to preschooler* ISBN 1876451 157

Kids Food Health 3: *From school-age to teenage* ISBN 1876451 165

For further information on these and all of our titles, visit our website: www.finch.com.au

Index

Page numbers in *italics* indicate photographs.